The United States Army W<

The United States Army War College educates and develops leaders for service at the strategic level while advancing knowledge in the global application of Landpower.

The purpose of the United States Army War College is to produce graduates who are skilled critical thinkers and complex problem solvers. Concurrently, it is our duty to the U.S. Army to also act as a "think factory" for commanders and civilian leaders at the strategic level worldwide and routinely engage in discourse and debate concerning the role of ground forces in achieving national security objectives.

The Strategic Studies Institute publishes national security and strategic research and analysis to influence policy debate and bridge the gap between military and academia.

The Center for Strategic Leadership contributes to the education of world class senior leaders, develops expert knowledge, and provides solutions to strategic Army issues affecting the national security community.

The Peacekeeping and Stability Operations Institute provides subject matter expertise, technical review, and writing expertise to agencies that develop stability operations concepts and doctrines.

The School of Strategic Landpower develops strategic leaders by providing a strong foundation of wisdom grounded in mastery of the profession of arms, and by serving as a crucible for educating future leaders in the analysis, evaluation, and refinement of professional expertise in war, strategy, operations, national security, resource management, and responsible command.

The U.S. Army Heritage and Education Center acquires, conserves, and exhibits historical materials for use to support the U.S. Army, educate an international audience, and honor soldiers—past and present.

STRATEGIC
STUDIES
INSTITUTE

The Strategic Studies Institute (SSI) is part of the U.S. Army War College and is the strategic-level study agent for issues related to national security and military strategy with emphasis on geostrategic analysis.

The mission of SSI is to use independent analysis to conduct strategic studies that develop policy recommendations on:

- Strategy, planning, and policy for joint and combined employment of military forces;

- Regional strategic appraisals;

- The nature of land warfare;

- Matters affecting the Army's future;

- The concepts, philosophy, and theory of strategy; and,

- Other issues of importance to the leadership of the Army.

Studies produced by civilian and military analysts concern topics having strategic implications for the Army, the Department of Defense, and the larger national security community.

In addition to its studies, SSI publishes special reports on topics of special or immediate interest. These include edited proceedings of conferences and topically oriented roundtables, expanded trip reports, and quick-reaction responses to senior Army leaders.

The Institute provides a valuable analytical capability within the Army to address strategic and other issues in support of Army participation in national security policy formulation.

Strategic Studies Institute
and
U.S. Army War College Press

STRATEGY AND GRAND STRATEGY:
WHAT STUDENTS AND PRACTITIONERS NEED
TO KNOW

Tami Davis Biddle

December 2015

*****

Comments pertaining to this report are invited and should be forwarded to: Director, Strategic Studies Institute and U.S. Army War College Press, U.S. Army War College, 47 Ashburn Drive, Carlisle, PA 17013-5010.

*****

All Strategic Studies Institute (SSI) and U.S. Army War College (USAWC) Press publications may be downloaded free of charge from the SSI website. Hard copies of certain reports may also be obtained free of charge while supplies last by placing an order on the SSI website. Check the website for availability. SSI publications may be quoted or reprinted in part or in full with permission and appropriate credit given to the U.S. Army Strategic Studies Institute and U.S. Army War College Press, U.S. Army War College, Carlisle, PA. Contact SSI by visiting our website at the following address: *www.StrategicStudiesInstitute.army.mil.*

*****

The Strategic Studies Institute and U.S. Army War College Press publishes a monthly email newsletter to update the national security community on the research of our analysts, recent and forthcoming publications, and upcoming conferences sponsored by the Institute. Each newsletter also provides a strategic commentary by one of our research analysts. If you are interested in receiving this newsletter, please subscribe on the SSI website at *www.StrategicStudiesInstitute.army.mil/newsletter.*

FOREWORD

There is no word or phrase more important and essential to the national security community than "strategy." In this monograph, Dr. Tami Davis Biddle argues that, while most of us have a sense of what the word means, we do not always fully appreciate all that it entails and all that it demands of us. Indeed, she argues that because strategy is so difficult on so many levels, we must not delude ourselves into believing that it can be practiced in any idealized form. But she insists that in situations where lives are at stake, we have a moral obligation to do all we can to meet the wide array of challenges we must face as we devise and implement strategies (and grand strategies) to achieve desired political ends.

Dr. Biddle begins her monograph with a close examination of the terms "strategy" and "grand strategy." Relying on a wide body of literature by historians, political scientists, and practitioners, she examines the reasons why political actors adopt strategies and grand strategies, and she helps us understand how the terms have been used—and have evolved—over time. She observes that the way in which strategies and grand strategies have been developed and implemented by actors in the international system has followed a narrative arc determined largely by the changing character, over time, of social, political, and military organizations.

Relying on this definitional and historical groundwork, Dr. Biddle articulates the myriad reasons why the practice of strategy is such a difficult and demanding art. She argues that strategy requires a logic that can be explained and defended, but points out that often this logic rests on assumptions that have not been thoroughly and rigorously examined. She argues that, even when the logic of strategy makes sense, its implementation will be eroded and undermined by contending interests and bureaucratic politics; unforeseen and unanticipated events; the pressures of domestic politics; the limits of human cognition, attention, and endurance; and the ongoing challenges posed by civil-military interaction.

Dr. Biddle's clear-headed examination of strategy, which is full of useful examples and sober guidance, will sharpen the analytical skills and deepen the situational awareness of students and practitioners alike.

DOUGLAS C. LOVELACE, JR.
Director
Strategic Studies Institute and
U.S. Army War College Press

ABOUT THE AUTHOR

TAMI DAVIS BIDDLE is Professor of National Security at the U.S. Army War College (USAWC), in Carlisle, PA. She was the Hoyt S. Vandenberg Professor of Aerospace Studies at the USAWC from 2011-13. Prior to that, she was the 2005-07 George C. Marshall Professor of Military Studies at the USAWC and the 2001-02 Harold K. Johnson Visiting Professor of Military History at the U.S. Army's Military History Institute. Before coming to the USAWC, she taught in the Department of History at Duke University, where she was a core faculty member of the Duke-University of North Carolina Joint Program in Military History. She is a member of the Board of Trustees of the Society for Military History. Dr. Biddle's research focus has been warfare in the 20th century, in particular the history of air warfare. She also studies and writes about military organization and leadership, civil-military relations, grand strategy, national security policy, and professional military education. Dr. Biddle's book, *Rhetoric and Reality in Air Warfare: The Evolution of British and American Ideas about Strategic Bombing, 1914-1945* (Princeton, NJ: Princeton University Press, 2002) was a Choice Outstanding Academic Title for 2002 and was added to the Chief of Air Staff's Reading List, Royal Air Force. Recently, she wrote the chapter on strategic bombing for the *Cambridge History of the Second World War* (2015). Other publication credits include: "Leveraging Strength: The Pillars of American Grand Strategy in World War II" in *Orbis*, Winter 2011; "Dresden 1945: Reality, History, and Memory," in *The Journal of Military History*, Vol. 72, No. 2 (April 2008); and "The Role of Military History in the Contemporary Academy," a *Society for Military History White Paper* (2014), written with Robert M. Citino. Dr. Biddle has held fellowships from Harvard, the Social Science Research Council, and the Smithsonian Institution's National Air and Space Museum, and she holds a Ph.D. in history from Yale University.

SUMMARY

In this monograph, Dr. Tami Davis Biddle examines why it is so difficult to devise, implement, and sustain sound strategies and grand strategies. Her analysis begins with an examination of the meaning of the term "strategy" and a history of the ways that political actors have sought to employ strategies and grand strategies to achieve their desired political aims. She examines the reasons why the logic undergirding strategy is often lacking and why challenges of implementation (including bureaucratic politics, unforeseen events, civil-military tensions, and domestic pressures) complicate and undermine desired outcomes. This clear-headed critique, built on a broad base of literature (historical and modern; academic and policy-oriented), will serve as a valuable guide to students and policymakers alike as they seek to navigate their way through the unavoidable challenges—and inevitable twists and turns—inherent in the development and implementation of strategy.

.

STRATEGY AND GRAND STRATEGY: WHAT STUDENTS AND PRACTITIONERS NEED TO KNOW

Tami Davis Biddle

The contemporary word "strategy" came to us from ancient Greece, where it referred to the art or skill of the general. In this original iteration, it was closer to what we now call "tactics."[1] The word has evolved over time and has been subjected to stretching and pulling. It has been appropriated by a wide range of actors—many of whom have had little or nothing to do with either the military or national security. Indeed, the word "strategy" is so widely used today that one may see it applied to everything from warfighting to the marketing of beverages.[2] Often it is used as a substitute or synonym for the rather more basic term "plan." Moreover, there is no standard contemporary definition of the term (or the related phrase "grand strategy") embraced by those who write about national security and international affairs. Even within this realm, there are definitional differences that vary by discipline and reference group. For instance, political scientists often use the phrase "grand strategy" to discuss what historians might refer to, instead, as a general framework for foreign policy, such as neo-isolationism, selective engagement, or primacy.[3]

Because this lack of consensus can lead to confusion, it is essential for scholars or practitioners who study and/or work in the realm of international security to articulate their own definition of the terms "strategy" and "grand strategy," or to select from among the many available in the existing literature. Students of international security need to think hard about the history and meaning of strategy, and reflect on what it demands of the practitioner. Students who proceed beyond academic study and attempt to practice the art of strategy will quickly gain a healthy respect for the myriad challenges it poses.

The purpose of this monograph is to give the student of strategy an anchor point—a foothold that can be used as a foundation for further analysis and primer for work in the practical realm. After offering definitions that I find helpful, I explain why political actors traditionally have sought to develop strategies and grand strategies to guide their behavior in the international system. I then examine the evolution of strategy and grand strategy in history. Finally, and most importantly, I examine the myriad challenges one must face in developing and implementing strategy and grand strategy. These challenges exist for many reasons, not the least of them being that strategy demands a theory—a proposed causal explanation—that must stand up to rigorous analysis. A theory, in its most basic form, can be expressed as: "if x, then y." Thus, the strategist must be able to defend the statement, "If we use resource X, then we will achieve objective Y" ("or at least move in the direction of achieving objective Y"). But the word "then" carries a heavy burden since it must be able to do a lot of work and bear intense evaluation—and this scrutiny must include, **above all**, the close examination of one's assumptions since these serve as the building blocks of the causal relationship linking ends and means. Strategy rests on assumptions; if assumptions go unexamined, then one risks building a strategic edifice on a foundation of sand.[4]

Often, however, such scrutiny does not take place, either because no one takes the time for it or because it would question or challenge organizational culture or individual preferences. Too often, the explanatory logic of strategy ends up being little more than an organizational mantra, or a facile assertion about the overwhelming power of a particular military instrument, or the easy opportunity presented by an enemy's presumed frailties. When faced with an unanticipated crisis, political decisionmakers may grab for the first option that looks even vaguely plausible in order to keep domestic critics at bay—especially those who would charge them with being unresponsive and/or weak. The laws of cognitive psychology will be at work (as they are in all human endeavors): the actors involved will "see what they want to see," filtering out disconfirming data or evidence that causes individual or institutional stress.[5]

A seasoned strategist knows that linking objectives and resources requires—indeed demands—doing homework. If, for instance, one wants to convince a rival state to make a concession, then one must assess (at a minimum) the stakes involved for both parties and the willingness of their populations to pay a price or endure sacrifices for the sake of the interest involved. One must assess the nature of the adversary, including its political and social composition and structure, the resiliency of that structure, and the robustness of its popular and elite will. One must understand the adversary's domestic politics, and the nature of the relationships between the population, the government, and the military.[6] Finally, one must assess one's own instruments of power available for persuasion and coercion—including whether or not they are available, acceptable, and well-suited to the purpose for which they will be used. These questions, though crucial, are only **a starting place** since each one raises additional questions to pose and answers to obtain. The work is painstaking and demanding, but the cost of shortcuts can be very high — even catastrophic.[7]

Even if one's assumptions are sound and if the logic of strategy makes sense on a fundamental level, many factors will intrude to erode or break the link between means and ends. These will include the challenges of communication inherent in complex enterprises; the adaptability of one's adversary; the complications of domestic politics; the stresses and strains of civil-military relations; and the unavoidable biases, predispositions, and limitations of the agencies attempting to implement the strategy.[8]

The student of strategy who also seeks to become an effective practitioner of this difficult art must prepare to develop such qualities as patience, empathy, judgment, and, above all, the resilience and determination to rebound from the inevitable and repeated setbacks that are inherent in the enterprise. Paul Kennedy has pointed out, perceptively, that grand strategy in particular relies upon "the constant and intelligent reassessment of . . . means and ends; it relies upon wisdom and judgment."[9]

WORDS AND MEANINGS

Within the military, there is a hierarchy of terms that define and delineate specific activities related to tactics and strategy; they are nested like a set of Russian dolls, with each one referring to a particular band of action and responsibility. They begin with "tactics" at the lowest level, and move upward and outward to "grand strategy" at the highest level. Because these terms must be comprehended and used consistently by large groups of people, they have official definitions and are incorporated into formal service doctrine. In general, "tactics" describe how small units (platoons, companies, ships, and squadrons) are to be employed in a battle space. Moving up one notch, "operations" (and "operational art") concern the movement of larger military units, including army divisions, naval task forces, and wings of aircraft. "Theater strategy" concerns the direction of the largest military units in a battle space, including armies and army groups, naval fleets, and numbered air forces.[10] Theater strategy (also referred to as military strategy) "prescribes how military instruments per se are to achieve the goals set for them by grand strategy within a given theater of war."[11] At the top of the definitional hierarchy, "grand strategy" identifies and articulates a given political actor's security objectives at a particular point in time and describes how they will be achieved using a **combination** of instruments of power—including military, diplomatic, and economic instruments. John Lewis Gaddis has described grand strategy as "the calculated relationship of means to large ends. It's about how one uses whatever one has to get to wherever it is one wants to go."[12]

In an effort to clarify these relationships, noted historian Samuel Eliot Morison wrote many years ago that:

> General Lee's decision to cross the Potomac into Maryland in 1862 was strategy, but the manner in which he fought General McClellan at Antietam was tactics. The British decision in 1942 to hang on in the desert west of Egypt was a matter of strategy; whilst General Montgomery's directives for the Battle of El Alamein, and the execution thereof, were tactical.

Morison added that "Bad strategy can render the most brilliant tactics fruitless . . . Conversely, sound tactics are necessary to implement good strategy."[13]

Theater strategy and grand strategy form the backbone of the curriculum at senior staff colleges inside the U.S. military's professional military education system, where practitioners study the many elements shaping the highest level of their art. Faculty members at these colleges understand and use the word "strategy" in roughly similar ways.[14] They perceive its central idea as the intelligent identification, utilization, and coordination of resources (ways and means) for the successful attainment of a specific objective (end).[15] While this sentence implies a direct and easily comprehended relationship, the simplicity is deceptive. Barriers to creating a straightforward linkage between ends, ways, and means are not only very real, but also multifaceted and persistent. This fact poses challenges for the way that strategy and grand strategy is taught in an academic setting. A framework that uses "ends, ways, and means" is not a bad way to enter into a discussion of strategy since it gives students a chance to gain initial traction as they begin their analysis. However, it is not enough to simply posit a calculated relationship between ends and means, assuming that optimal means and ends can be readily identified and that the relationship between utilizing a particular resource (or combination of them) and achieving a political aim will be straightforward, easily articulated, or uncomplicated to implement.

Recently, the teaching of strategy in the professional military education system has been criticized on the ground that it fails to capture the complexities of the way that strategy and grand strategy are created and implemented in the real world. A RAND study led by Linda Robinson argued the U.S. military is taught to expect a linear approach in which the policymakers provide the objectives and the military develops the options for achieving them.[16] Instead, the authors argue, "Civilian policymakers require an active dialogue with the military and other sources of information to inform the diagnosis of the situation, as well as to develop realistic policy objectives." The authors add that there is a need for an "established integrated civilian-military process that would rigorously identify assumptions, risks, possible outcomes, and second-order effects through soliciting diverse inputs, red-teaming, and table-top exercises."[17]

The argument raises some important questions about how one identifies civilian and military roles in a system shaped by what Samuel Huntington called 'objective control' of the military, which requires a delineation between civilian and military realms of professional competence.[18] But the critique is surely an important one that ought to inform pedagogy, not only in the professional military education (PME) system, but also beyond. Military and civilian leaders need to comprehend one another's professional realms well enough to be able to work together to produce coherent strategy. On the military side, officers must acquire political acumen without political assertiveness. They must understand the political environment they work in well enough to be effective while resisting any temptation toward political meddling.[19] This is a non-trivial challenge, but it is central to sound civil-military relations and to the kind of strategy that such relations make possible.[20]

Robinson and her co-authors are right to argue that civilian authorities are unlikely to frame political objectives with precision or clarity – or even timeliness. Instead, objectives will develop iteratively (and often haltingly) in response to events, contingencies, and perceived options. In some cases, civilian authorities may wish to be presented with military options **before** they commit themselves to preferred objectives.[21] Thus, military planners must abandon the belief that they will always be able to build a strategy that is designed or tailored to meet a well-articulated political objective. However much military leaders may seek clarity and specific goals, political leaders will seek options, possibilities, and flexibility. While this may be frustrating for military leaders, it is far better for them to recognize the realities than to base their expectations on an idealized form of the process that exists only in the antiseptic environment of the classroom.

Equally, civilian education largely has been inadequate in this realm. Civilians often fail to realize just how blunt an instrument military force is—and they fail to realize the many challenges of implementing it, not least the logistical challenges. This problem has been exacerbated by the creation of an all-volunteer force and the resulting marked division in American society between those who have military experience and those who do not. Those in the latter category simply do not have enough insight into military operations to understand how they can be used to attain political ends or to realize the limitations of their ability to do so.[22] This greatly complicates the civil-military dialogue that is the very heart of strategy making within a democratic polity. The problem is surely exacerbated by the lack of opportunities for civilians to gain even a basic understanding of military operations and strategy. Aside from well-developed programs at Yale and Columbia—and similarly strong programs at a few other universities—strategy (especially as it relates to military operations) is rarely a topic of serious and sustained examination in the civilian academy in the United States.[23] This is unfortunate since the stakes, and therefore the costs of failure, are high—measurable directly in national blood and treasure.

STRATEGY AND THE INTERNATIONAL SYSTEM

Any political actor operating in the international system has a set of interests it seeks to defend and advance through the utilization of its available resources. These actors (whether the city-states and empires of the past, or the states and nonstate actors of the present) are willing to expend resources to protect and further those interests in a system wherein neither success nor survival is guaranteed. If we link this observation to strategy, we can see that interests relate to ends, and resources relate to ways and means.[24] If they are sufficient in quality and quantity, an actor's resources can serve as "instruments of power"—leverage mechanisms—that can help it to sustain itself, and perhaps even thrive, in a competitive and often dangerous world.[25] Historian and analyst Sir Michael Howard has observed that:

> The objective of most states most of the time is always to maintain their independence, often to extend their influence, and sometimes to extend their dominion. The classical tools at their disposal have been three: armed force, wealth, and allies.[26]

States that seek to hold great sway over the international system (its structure and functioning) may be willing to expend considerable resources to shape it in a particular way; this was the case for Britain in the era of the *Pax Britannica,* and it is true of the United States today.

Usable resources come in many forms; military might is only one way for state actors to attain the ends they seek. For instance, actors can leverage knowledge and education—as Britain did in World War II—creating a scientific and academic brain trust that made immeasurable contributions to the battle with Hitler's Germany.[27] Smaller states like Canada, Denmark, and Singapore have been able to achieve strategic goals through the development of strong relationships with larger neighbors, and, in each case, the development of a reputation for stability and predictability in domestic and global affairs.

The instruments of power that a political actor can wield—and the complexity of the interactions among them—varies with the basic resources available to it, and the degree of social, economic, political, and scientific advancement it has attained. But the nature of the international system matters greatly since the tools at an actor's disposal are influenced by the nature of the system. Armed force, because it enables an actor to protect its territory and possessions, typically has been considered the ultimate guarantee of existence in an anarchical system. But a powerful indigenous military is not always necessary for success; indeed, in many cases, military power is not the best tool for the attainment of political aims. For instance, post-World War II Japan relied on its close ties with the United States to protect its territorial integrity and regional interests. This enabled Japan to develop internally and to focus its energy on education, economic development, and nondefense production. These activities, in turn, created wealth—and wealth offered Japan another instrument of power with which to determine its subsequent fate.

Prior to World War II, the British, relying in particular on their powerful navy, structured and preserved a particular global order that served Britain's interests and underwrote a system of international trade. In the 20th century—and in particular after World War II—the United States created a network of institutions that served its interests, but also facilitated the international interaction of states; it offered incentives for actors to buy into the U.S.-preferred system and seek the advantages to be gained by working within its economic, legal, and political frameworks.[28] Smaller states that took advantage of the system could in fact gain outsized influence within it. Challengers to U.S. hegemony have sought (and will continue to seek) to utilize their resources to sway the system in a direction of their own preference. The system as it exists is guaranteed by U.S. willingness to spend resources, including force, to preserve it. Therefore, strategy, as it applies to the behavior of political actors, can never be considered **wholly** without reference to military power.[29]

As we noted previously, the word "strategy" had its roots squarely within the military realm. In a seminal article on strategy written in 2000, Professor Richard K. Betts argued:

> Strategy is the essential ingredient for making war either politically effective or morally tenable. It is the link between military means and political ends, the scheme for how to make one produce the other. Without strategy, there is no rationale for how force will achieve purposes worth the price in blood and treasure.[30]

This is among the most powerful and perceptive definitions of strategy ever written, and it is one that military officers and national security professionals must take to heart and never forget. It links strategy and military force, and it underscores the fact that when armed force is involved, strategy includes an inherent, undeniable moral component.

The modern international system affords a wide array of tools that political actors can employ to attain the political ends they seek; these include, among others, wealth and economic leverage, information and moral suasion, and diplomacy. Thus, most contemporary authors are willing to employ the word "strategy" even when military power is in the background rather than the foreground. But the demands of strategy and strategic decisionmaking are just as high in these instances as they are in the military realm, even if the cost of failure may not be quite so acute.[31] Every time an individual instrument of power is used, it must have a logic that informs how means will produce ends. That scheme must be robust enough to stand up to critical thinking and aggressive analytical scrutiny—and it must be resilient enough to endure unforeseen events, unanticipated barriers, failures of imagination, and the natural complications of human interaction and communication.

The situation grows more complex when **multiple** instruments are employed simultaneously to address a serious and sustained problem. In this circumstance, it is usually appropriate to use the phrase "grand strategy." In his book *The Strategy Bridge*, Colin Gray defines grand strategy as "the direction and use made of any or all of the assets of a security community, including its military instrument, for the purposes of policy as decided by politics."[32] In the journal of Britain's Royal United Services Institute, Peter Layton explained that:

The essence of grand strategy is its integrative nature. In a conceptual sense grand strategy is a system: a set of interdependent elements where change in some elements . . . produces change across the system, and the entire system exhibits properties and behaviours different from the constituent parts.[33]

This echoes what historian Paul Kennedy noted a generation earlier, when he described grand strategy as a "complex and multi-layered thing" that demands the intelligent interaction of all of a nation's significant resources, in order to achieve a desired political end.[34] It echoes, as well, elements of Betts' argument that "strategies are chains of relationships among means and ends that span several levels of analysis, from the maneuvers of units in specific engagements through larger campaigns, whole wars, grand strategies, and foreign policies."[35]

The first requirement of strategy (and grand strategy) is that it be physically possible and economically feasible. Any practitioner will quickly come to understand that strategy is unavoidably and ineluctably about trade-offs. Even in wealthy nations, resources are limited; this fact demands that one choose carefully and wisely from the available set. The second requirement of strategy is that it must be acceptable — morally and culturally — to the people who will implement it. If it fails this test, it will not be sustainable over time. Finally, it must be sensibly matched to the problem (or set of problems) at hand; in other words, it must be well-suited to solving the problem it is meant to address. Failure in any one of these categories will mean failure overall.[36] Because these fundamentals are so important, military and civilian students in the U.S. professional military education system are taught to subject any potential strategy to a "FAS test," which is an acronym for feasibility, acceptability, and suitability.[37]

These criteria are much more complex than they may appear on first glance. Knowing whether a strategy is "suitable" requires knowing a great deal about the problem one is trying to solve; similarly, one must realize that conditions are not static: what is acceptable to one's own population early in a conflict may not be acceptable later—or vice versa. Hew Strachan has observed that:

> If strategy is a matter of combining means, ways, and ends, what are the ends towards which a state . . . is aiming when it cannot be precise about the future context within which its means and ways are being applied?

He adds:

> Answering that question is the central conundrum of grand strategy, and being able to do so sensibly is correspondingly more difficult the more extended the definition of the future which grand strategy uses.[38]

Strategy, unavoidably, involves moving forward from a starting point (rarely an ideal one) and then constantly reassessing the situation in light of changing conditions. This requires an ongoing monitoring of the relationship between ends and means. In wartime, this demands constant reassessment in light of enemy moves and the unanticipated twists and turns that develop in the ongoing presence of what Carl von Clausewitz termed "friction."[39] In 1940, Britain's wartime strategy involved little more than near-term survival; by 1941, its policymakers were able to envision and shape the sweeping goals of the Atlantic Charter; and by 1943, it was able to announce, with Allied partners, a demand for the unconditional surrender of Germany and Japan.[40]

During the 20th century—in the era of the two World Wars and later during the Cold War—the phrase "grand strategy" came into frequent and common usage. In his classic 1954 book *Strategy*, historian and military analyst Sir Basil Liddell Hart explained that, "As tactics is an application of strategy on a lower plane, so strategy is an application on a lower plane of 'grand strategy.'" The role of the latter, he explained, "is to coordinate and direct all the resources of a nation, or band of nations, towards the attainment of the political object of the war."[41] Both Liddell Hart and Morison saw the phrases "grand strategy" and "higher strategy" as synonymous.[42]

Other prominent authors, writing in the same era, had begun to envision "grand strategy" as a phrase that was relevant and applicable in both wartime and peacetime. In the first (1943) edition of the classic text, *Makers of Modern Strategy*, editor Edward Meade Earle set forward elegant definitions of strategy and grand strategy that were descriptive **and** normative:

> Strategy is the art of controlling and utilizing the resources of a nation—or a coalition of nations—including its armed forces, to the end that its vital interests shall be effectively promoted and secured against enemies, actual, potential, or merely presumed. The highest type of strategy—sometimes called 'grand strategy'—is that which so integrates the policies and armaments of the nation that the resort to war is either rendered unnecessary or is undertaken with the maximum chance of victory.[43]

Earle did not restrict either "strategy" or "grand strategy" to the wielding of military power alone, but placed them squarely within the framework of international security and related them directly to the making of war and the preservation of peace. Earle's integrated definition of strategy and grand strategy asked that one draw intelligently from a broad but not inexhaustible resource base, structuring and coordinating those resources as efficiently and effectively as possible to facilitate the realization of discernable endpoints that have been articulated by legitimate authorities and have won general support. With respect to grand strategy in particular, he offered an overarching conceptualization of an ideal—but an ideal that is inherently demanding and difficult to achieve.

In a lecture to the U.S. Naval War College in 1952, Liddell Hart told students that, where warfare is concerned, grand strategy must take a long view—"for its problem is the winning of the peace."[44] In this, he was surely right. Any actors seeking to attain political aims through warfighting must think hard about how those aims will facilitate a better, more stable peace than the one that preceded the fighting.[45] Additionally, they must think hard, and with unflinching realism, about how the potential costs of war (by every measure) will stack up against the potential gains.

Not infrequently, actors will opt for the use of military power when other instruments might have been better suited to achieving the political aim. The seduction of military force lies in its promise (rarely if ever attained) for straightforward gains over a relatively short time period and at minimal cost. In some cases, those who believe themselves to be bold and visionary leaders assume that, by wielding force, they can sidestep the normal complexities of diplomacy and political interaction. In other cases, military force seems like the quickest and most satisfactory way to answer an insult that has produced a domestic clamor. But hasty, ill-conceived, or purely emotional uses of force can prove disastrous.[46]

Wilhelmine Germany almost certainly would have attained most of its political objectives in the early years of the 20th century if it had avoided a reliance on military power (which helped trigger World War I). Indeed, Howard has argued that:

> Germany's growing wealth and productivity would eventually by itself have dominated the continent and gained her all the allies she needed. She could have acquired the status of World Power without having to fight for it.[47]

It is not at all unusual for actors to opt for the use of force based on fallacious assumptions about enemy will and determination. Sometimes a "quick" victory on the battlefield is perceived as a relatively painless way of resolving a problem, but there are only a few historical instances in which warfighting has been either quick or painless. In many cases, the outcome achieved is only loosely aligned with the original end sought. Actors frequently are poor judges of their own vital interests. Indeed, despite a widespread view that land wars in Asia were to be avoided, U.S. decision-makers nonetheless were lured into a long and costly fight in Vietnam in part because of an often-repeated but superficial mantra that had gained traction in domestic discourse, "the domino theory."[48] Fearing that his ambitious domestic agenda would be jeopardized if he did not look sufficiently tough in the realm of foreign policy, President Lyndon B. Johnson thrust the American military into a post-colonial conflict that they did not understand and were poorly equipped to address.[49] Writing at the height of the Vietnam War, Bernard Brodie addressed the U.S. identification of interests in scathing but highly perceptive terms:

> Vital interests, despite common assumptions to the contrary, have only a vague connection with objective fact. A sovereign nation determines for itself what its vital interests are (freedom to do so is what the term "sovereign" means) and its leaders accomplish this exacting task largely by using their highly fallible and inevitably biased human judgment to interpret the external political environment.[50]

Additionally, a political actor's ends will very rarely, if ever, align completely with its allies' preferred ends. These differences between allies will likely become more acute as a war progresses and moves towards a termination phase.[51] Allies may share one or two overarching objectives, but they are likely to differ over the nature of more specific ends and the methods required to achieve them. These differences can be acute and troublesome. Americans, due to their nature and culture, have a particularly hard time accepting that others do not want the same things that they want. In a perceptive essay on the North Atlantic Treaty Organization (NATO) war in Afghanistan, Antulio Echevarria observed presciently that in the absence of "genuine existential threats," states may prefer to muddle through a war than to embrace a robust and coherent grand strategy that requires serious compromise over domestic preference and long-term interests.[52]

Liddell Hart's insistence on "winning the peace" also demands that soldiers and statesmen bear in mind that, in most cases, the hardest work comes **after** battles have been fought. Soldiers remain crucial here, since they provide whatever ongoing coercive leverage the victorious side may need to secure armistice terms and to provide the basic security required to facilitate all other projects within the defeated actor's territorial realm, including political development and humanitarian assistance. The moment marking the transition from "war" to "post-war," can be particularly fraught and dangerous since it is especially demanding of civil-military cooperation. Seams that are not stitched carefully will allow the (often fragile) fabric to tear and fray.[53]

STRATEGY IN HISTORY

A brief look into the past enables one to understand the layers of complexity inherent in strategy and grand strategy. Moreover, it allows one to see how they have evolved over time in relation to changes in politics, socio-economics, and technology. Finally, while one must be careful with the too readily wielded phrase "strategic culture," history does allow us to perceive some national proclivities and tendencies in the strategic behavior of particular states.[54]

The high level of civilization achieved by the ancient Greeks led to their wielding power in ways that seem familiar and "modern" to us today. But this changed with the coming of a feudal order in Europe; not until the late-18th century would that modernity reappear in full form, in particular with the return of "the people" — and popular will — as a key element of strategic calculation. The political and industrial revolutions of the late-18th century, the reemergence of democracy as a powerful political idea, and the rise of mass communications changed the landscape of strategic decisionmaking fundamentally. These changes placed a new emphasis on civil-military relations: the requirements of "representative government" meant that decisions about the wielding of military and coercive force would be in the hands of elected officials who, unlike their military counterparts, would face sanction at the ballot box if their strategies failed or lost popular support. But these civilian decisionmakers nonetheless had to rely on the professional expertise and skill of a trained military.[55]

As noted at the beginning of the monograph, the ancient Greeks gave us the root of the modern English word "strategy," but their own use of the term was more akin to our modern word for "tactics" — movements on a battlefield.[56] Still, the Greece of Socrates and Aristophanes was advanced enough in its politics to engage in activities that required strategy and grand strategy (in their modern conception).[57] We can, for instance, identify the latter in the plan that Pericles developed for war with Sparta. Resting on a set of assumptions about the dominance of Athenian naval power, the security provided to citizens by the Athenian long walls, and the unwillingness of the conservative Spartans to engage in a protracted campaign, Pericles imagined and articulated a strategy that he believed finally would secure full respect for the rising Athenian state. He linked Athenian ways and means to an end he desired and expected (wrongly, in the end) to be achievable at acceptable cost.[58]

At about the same time in history, albeit in a different part of the world, the warring states of ancient China used strategy to maintain their survival in a highly competitive environment. Sun-Tzu's articulation of strategic principles, which would ultimately be collected in a volume that modern readers know as *The Art of War*, continues to be studied carefully by students of strategy around the world.[59]

We can discern strategy, as well, in the empire building of ancient Rome. The Romans were able to use a heavy reliance on military power to build a vast empire, despite their possession of few natural resources. Constant exposure to external danger helped mold a society that elevated martial values, honored military skill, and made military service a central element of citizenship. Thus, Rome could field formidable armies, and the Roman polity could endure high casualties without changing its political aims. The ability of the Romans to extract such manpower resources enabled them to create and sustain a far-flung empire that was a vehicle for the extension of Roman influence.[60]

Europe of the Middle Ages had specific legal, social, and military structures centered on the obligations between vassals and overlords.[61] Interactions among political actors rested on diplomacy (including marriage arrangements), economic leverage, and the work of feudal armies. Eventually, the development of firearms and artillery contributed to shifts driven principally by the expansion of a money economy: wealthy overlords increasingly could use payments to secure the services of those who would protect their interests militarily.[62] The deft combination of missile fire and rapid movement demonstrated so well at Agincourt in 1415 was replaced over time by large formations of musket and pike. Limited in their communications and dependent on fixed points of supply, these formations were lumbering and sluggish. Heavy reliance on mercenaries contributed to the ossification of strategy and the indecisive nature of war in this era. Even when they were generally competent, mercenaries were prone to desertion and mutiny unless they were promptly paid and supplied; most states found them "unreliable and often dangerous to their employers."[63]

By the early-16th century, the problem of raising and wielding an army for the purposes of the state attracted renewed attention, spurring a revival of interest in the military methods of the classical civilizations—and in particular in the linkage between citizenship and soldiery. Machiavelli's *Arte della guerra* (*The Art of War*), emphasizing training and hierarchical command, was the most notable of many treatises that turned for inspiration to the Greco-Roman military system. The "new laws of warfare" that Machiavelli sought to distill for contemporary use were, in fact, "the old laws of the Roman military order."[64]

Machiavelli fundamentally believed that to conquer and expand were the natural tendencies of man; therefore, he believed that war "was the most essential activity of political life."[65] In this quintessentially realist conception of international affairs, he developed a utilitarian idea of war and politics that pulled away from more traditional ethical considerations and made his name odious to later generations. But he had edged in the direction of modern social science by relating warfare to economic and political imperatives; he sought, as well, to "enlarge the realm of human planning and to reduce the field of chance."[66]

Working at the University of Leiden between 1571 and 1591, philosopher Justus Lipsius—an admirer of Machiavelli—perceived war not "as an act of uncontrolled violence, but rather the orderly application of force, directed by a competent and legitimate authority, in the interest of the state." This perspective helped drive the Dutch reforms enacted by the princes of the House of Orange-Nassau to create a new model army. Inspired by the example of the Romans, these long-service professionals were "reasonably efficient instruments of state policy, responding in a predictable pattern of obedience to the orders of a defined political-military chain of command."[67]

Gustavus Adolphus of Sweden and Raimundo Montecuccoli of the Austrian Hapsburgs were both admirers of the Dutch reformers.[68] Montecuccoli was responsible for the first systematic effort, in the early modern era, to address war in all its dimensions — including its administrative, political, and social dimensions. This intellectual heritage was passed on to the Duke of Marlborough in Great Britain and Frederick the Great in Prussia. Subsequently, it influenced thought and action during the French Revolution and the Prussian reformers who responded to it, including Gerhard von Scharnhorst and Clausewitz.[69]

Overall, the 17th century reformers had enlarged armies and placed renewed emphasis on discipline, drill, chains of command, and orderly administration. They had sought to make armies into true instruments of foreign policy. But they worked in a dynastic era when warfare was a clash between rulers rather than peoples. A hereditary class of officers oversaw a mass of soldiers who were drawn from the less productive classes and who lived largely apart from the citizenry. Kept on a short leash, soldiers employed tactics that were mechanistic and routine-based; to send them on distant reconnaissance missions was to risk losing them to desertion. While they could be effective instruments *en masse*, they were not trusted as individuals. It was often difficult for a commander to bring battle against an unwilling enemy.[70]

A Revolution in War and Strategy.

As historian R. R. Palmer has noted, the period between the ascendance to power of Frederick the Great in 1740 and the final defeat of French General Napoleon Bonaparte in 1815 saw not only the increasing perfection of the dynastic form of war under Frederick, but also the dramatic influence of an entirely new form, as manifested in the French Revolution.[71] That historical turning point, which mirrored at least some of the ideas and forms of the earlier American Revolution, changed the nature of the relationship between a people and their government—and thereby changed what was possible in the military realm.

Strachan has argued that the idea of strategy derived from "the growth of standing professional armies on the one hand and of the Enlightenment on the other"; it is surely true that much of what we recognize in our contemporary notion of strategy finds its provenance in this 18th century convergence.[72] Strachan cites the work of Paul Gideon Joly de Maizeroy as signaling a decisive shift towards the modern. In his *Theorie de la guerre* (1777), Joly de Maizeroy argued that warmaking involved reflection, foresight, and reasoning:

> In order to formulate plans, strategy studies the relationship between time, positions, means, and different interests, and takes every factor into account ... which is the province of dialectics, that is to say, of reasoning, which is the highest faculty of the mind.[73]

Facing a conservative coalition of European powers in 1793, the revolutionary French Republic created the Committee on Public Safety to arrange for the security of the French people. Unfettered by the limits that had bound the dynastic rulers, the committee aroused the population, called for a general draft (the *levee en masse*), and imposed a war economy. Napoleon took full advantage of these opportunities to shock and overwhelm the opponents he faced. In 1799, Napoleon became the leading autocrat of France, and a year later he destroyed the Second Coalition arrayed against him through his decisive victory at the battle of Marengo, Italy. At the head of large armies fired by revolutionary zeal, Napoleon was able to part company with more limited forms of warfare. Though he worked with familiar tools — infantry, artillery, and cavalry — he was able to employ them with new levels of sophistication. He could take advantage of maneuver, reconnaissance, and exploitation in ways that his opponents could not. When a Third European Coalition was formed, Napoleon again humiliated them at Ulm and Austerlitz, Austria, in 1805.[74]

In addition to tactical genius, Napoleon exploited planning skills, administrative excellence, and superior staff work. All these were enhanced by the new meritocracy that opened command positions to those outside the hereditary classes.[75] In this, he sought to reduce the element of chance in battle and to elevate the significance of strategy — the considered linking of ways and means with political aims. Ultimately, Napoleon's vast political ambitions would catalyze enough military power — among those states trying to balance against him — to bring about his defeat on the battlefield.

As perceptive observer Heinrich Dietrich von Buelow noted, issues of military command began to overlap with those of diplomacy and domestic affairs: "under modern conditions of strategy there could be no separation between politics and war — great soldiers must understand foreign affairs, and successful diplomats must understand military action."[76] In this observation, we see the beginnings of a modern conception of that crucial element of modern strategy: sound civil-military relations. Von Buelow was surely correct to argue that generals and politicians needed to understand one another's work.

Strachan has observed that:

> Napoleon himself did not use the word strategy until he was exiled at St. Helena, but those who wrote about what he had achieved certainly did — not only Clausewitz, but also Jomini . . . and the Austrian Archduke Charles.[77]

An insistence on the linkage between politics and war would be, perhaps, the most important contribution of Napoleon's most important observer, Clausewitz. It was not the newness of Clausewitz's statement, but rather the forcefulness of its assertion that set Clausewitz apart: "His originality is not in his reassertion of what must really be an old idea but rather in the clarity and insistence with which he hews to it and develops it."[78] War, which makes sense only if it serves a political aim, is a political process conducted "with other means" — a process that analyst Thomas Schelling, writing in the mid-20th century, would describe as "vicious diplomacy."[79]

Published a year after his death in 1831, Clausewitz's *On War* remains the greatest effort ever made to understand the nature of war.[80] No doubt because he had faced so formidable an opponent as Napoleon, Clausewitz placed a heavy emphasis on the profound and sustained effort required to overcome friction in warfighting. Swiss writer Antoine Henri Jomini, who had fought alongside Napoleon and thus wrote from a different — and rather more optimistic — perspective, sought to identify and enumerate the scientific principles of warfighting that had enabled Napoleon to enjoy such dominance for nearly 2 decades. In large part because they seemed tangible and concrete — and thus seemed to offer the prospect of being reproducible in other situations — these principles would hold great appeal for many, especially in the 19th century. Jomini would have a deep influence, for instance, on the newly professionalizing U.S. Army, which had its intellectual roots in the discipline of engineering. John Shy has written perceptively that:

> Even across the Atlantic, Jomini was the leading interpreter of Napoleon and the dean of military theorists. . . . The younger, post-Napoleonic generation of officers was as impressed as its seniors by the value of reducing warfare to a handful of strategic maxims.[81]

While navies had long been crucial elements of state-based coercive leverage, the nature of their power as military and economic instruments was not fully articulated until the turn of the century when two talented theorists, Alfred Thayer Mahan of the United States and Sir Julian Corbett of Britain, put their observations and insights on paper. Mahan drew a linkage between maritime trade and national prosperity — and therefore between sea power and security. He also drew attention to the relationship between a state's geography and its strategic culture. Continental powers, surrounded by potentially hostile armies, had no choice but to focus the bulk of their attention on land power. But states freed by geography from the need for vigilant and expensive land-based defenses could develop cultures that highlighted individualism, capitalism, and the cosmopolitan outlook that comes with naval power and overseas trade. Both Corbett and

Mahan sought theories of grand strategy; for the latter, there was a "symbiotic link between sea power, liberal democracy and ideas of grand strategy." What Corbett called "major strategy" had "in its broadest sense to deal with the whole resources of the nation for war."[82]

In the early-20th century, the development of airplanes as powerful instruments of war highlighted the role of geography and culture in grand strategy. States with ongoing land-based threats tended to emphasize their armies and focus on air-land cooperation, while states like Britain and the United States had more freedom to think about air power as an independent coercive instrument, operating on its own to shape an enemy's incentives. The first main body of air power theory would develop during and after World War I, with its most public iterations issuing forth from the pens of Guilio Douhet, Sir Hugh Trenchard, and General Billy Mitchell. Writing after World War I, they promised — to those who would follow their advice — a restoration of offensive capabilities to warfighting and prompt, decisive victories. They warned of humiliating defeat for those who failed to exploit the potential of long-range bombardment to undermine an enemy's ability to fight and will to fight. These authors were not, however, as explicit as they might have been about the linkage — the exchange mechanism — between the employment of independent air power and the achievement of a desired political end. They did not tend to submit their work to the serious critical analysis necessary for sound strategic thinking; thus, their theories were notably underspecified. In addition, the technological challenges inherent in implementing air power as an independent instrument of war proved daunting.[83]

While air power would very quickly become an essential asset on the field of battle, its utility as an independent instrument capable of carrying out war-winning "strategic" bombing proved more elusive. If long-range bombing (in many forms and from many platforms) surely has been able to contribute to victory in past wars, its ability to do so independently has frequently fallen short of expectations and has been a source of ongoing debate and controversy. But the degree to which air power should be thought of as, or expected to be, an independent instrument is also a bone of contention. Throughout history, military forces that have been able to combine their many tools — intelligently and synergistically — have been the most successful. This fact did not change when air power appeared on the scene.

Strategy and Grand Strategy in the War-torn 20th Century.

By the late-19th century, political reforms and expansion of the franchise had extended the voice of the people in democratic states, and the growing circulation of newspapers to an increasingly literate public in Europe had heightened the volume and intensity of that voice. As Howard has noted, the role of public opinion had expanded over time:

> The mobilization of public opinion at home, the persuasion of opinion in neutral states, and the undermining of the legitimacy of the enemy government through propaganda, all became as much tools of grand strategy as the maintenance and deployment of armed forces, the preservation of a healthy economy, and the preservation of alliances.[84]

A revolution in sanitation and medicine had greatly increased the populations of European states, allowing for the possibility of vast conscripted armies. The rise of nationalism and a fiercely competitive environment in Europe, exacerbated by a second wave of aggressive colonialism, helped stoke embers that would erupt into an unprecedented conflagration.

When Europe plunged into war in 1914—just shy of 100 years after Napoleon's defeat—science, technology, economics, social relationships, and politics were all in the midst of rapid and unprecedented change. Industrialization and the widening array of highly lethal weapons had changed the nature of war forever (although neither soldiers nor civilians fully appreciated this fact prior to 1914). Other industrial processes, including mass production of everything from trucks to foodstuffs and clothing, would also affect the size of armies and the ways they could fight.[85] With all this happening at once, warfighting became a vastly larger and more daunting enterprise than it had ever been before in history. The need for nations to rationalize and organize their own resources fully, and to coordinate them with those of their allies, became acute, a matter of life and death.

The way in which different actors handled these changes affected their ability to leverage their strengths, compensate for their weaknesses, and link ways and means—both military and nonmilitary—to political objectives. World War I, which was the largest, costliest, and most complex conflagration that the world had ever seen, created a need for a grand strategic thought that was unprecedented in its range and scope. The states of the Entente (including Britain, France and, ultimately, the United States) fared better in the end than the Central Powers, anchored by the undemocratic Wilhelmine Germany and the fragile, fading Austro-Hungarian Empire. The grand strategy employed by the Allied Powers included the mass mobilization of state resources (human, industrial, technological, and scientific); information and propaganda campaigns, the extraction and leveraging of the resources of the British Empire; and the eventual attraction of American resources and American citizens to the cause. On behalf of political ideals, members of the Entente endured prolonged, brutal military campaigns on the Western Front and sustained an array of costly peripheral campaigns as well. Keeping their coalition together despite the loss of the Soviet ally in 1917, they revealed resilience and commitment to the goal of protecting democracy on the European continent. But the price was frightful, and the outcome of the war, detailed and articulated in the Treaty of Versailles and a set of related instruments, would unsettle world politics for the remainder of the 20th century and beyond.[86]

Deep German resentment of the Treaty of Versailles eventually would give Adolf Hitler running room to implement his vision for overturning the existing order and implementing a craven racialist ideology. The absence of the United States as a European security guarantor after the war, and the Anglo-French fear of facing another costly conflagration so soon after the last one, helped open doors for Hitler that otherwise might have been closed to him.[87]

In the end, Britain and France reluctantly decided that they had to stand up to Hitler's challenge to the international system. At the start of World War II, the survival of democratic principles and a capitalist economic structure for the developed world were once again in the balance. After France fell quickly, Prime Minister Winston Churchill realized Britain had little hope for a successful grand strategy in the absence of American help. But that help came slowly, first in the form of materiel, and then later in the form of a fully developed alliance with shared resources and knowledge.[88] In the interim, the democratic cause received an unexpected and ironic boost when Hitler invaded the Soviet Union.

Though American resources were partially diverted eastward after the Japanese attack on Pearl Harbor, HI, the Americans proved wealthy enough to fight on two fronts on opposite sides of the world. Once again, two democratic states, working in a loose but crucially important alliance with the Soviets, were able to prevail in the art of grand strategy. This was not done, however, without considerable difficulty and multiple setbacks along the way. Hitler's Third Reich was a formidable, adaptive foe that forced intelligent, effective, and sustained use of Allied resources. The energy of Allied grand strategy, and the glue that held it together, was the shared goal of defeating Hitler's heinous and exceptionally dangerous regime. Crafted in real time, Allied grand strategy was iterative; not infrequently, it was based on mistaken assumptions and judgments. Often it reflected the strains that stemmed from the different postwar hopes and visions of the United States, Britain, and the Soviet Union. But flawed as it was, it had strengths and advantages that Axis grand strategy simply did not possess.[89]

If we look specifically at American grand strategy in World War II, we can identify five central pillars of success. First, Americans built and sustained a functional civil-military relationship that facilitated all other activity. Second, they found ways to mobilize men and material, and to fight inside a democratic, capitalist paradigm that worked in concert with the nation's existing institutions. Third, the Americans leveraged the moral high ground ceded to them by their enemies and sustained national will by relying on mechanisms with well-established roots in the culture. Fourth, they used their ongoing relationship with the British to make better strategic choices than they might have made entirely on their own. Fifth, they embraced adaptability and resiliency, which allowed them to learn from their many mistakes and take advantage of their enemies' mistakes.[90]

However, the post-World War II environment proved to have little in common with the fondest hopes and aspirations of any of the combatants. The United States, which had emerged from the war largely unscathed and in a dominant economic position, found itself taking increasing responsibility for the liberal, capitalist world order that the Royal Navy had previously underwritten. But the Americans, much to their dismay, discovered that war against Hitler had not transformed the views and proclivities of the battered, distrustful Soviet leader. Josef Stalin's speech of February 9, 1946, made it clear that he did not expect any easy coexistence between communism and capitalism. A new environment entrenched as an "Iron Curtain" descended across central Europe.[91] The emergent Cold War brought an atmosphere of great mistrust, trapping the contending parties in an odd new realm between war and peace. Once the Soviets acquired nuclear weapons in 1949, the role of U.S. Armed Forces (and its allies around the world) became, more than ever, to **deter** wars rather than fight them.[92] The competitive structure of the postwar world also catalyzed a dramatic change in the disposition of the U.S. military. The creation of a permanent and well-resourced military organization raised the question of how that institution might be inserted into a liberal democratic political structure that held representative government ("government by the people and for the people") as its highest virtue.[93]

The U.S. grand strategy for coping with the communist threat—"containment," first authored by Soviet specialist George Kennan—sought to limit and circumscribe Soviet influence while avoiding warfighting; the Soviet system, Kennan believed, would ultimately collapse due to its own internal deficiencies and contradictions.[94] Kennan's original conception, developed in 1946-47, was hardened and sharpened when National Security Council Report Number 68, written principally by Paul Nitze, gained traction after the Korean War began in June 1950. As a result, vast resources moved to the Pentagon, which began to eclipse the State Department in power and influence. Both Kennan and Nitze had envisioned a grand strategy that brought myriad resources—including economic, diplomatic, and military—to bear, but Nitze's version of containment placed much more emphasis on military power than Kennan's.[95] In terms of our focus here, the main point is that the United States found it necessary to develop a grand strategy for a sustained engagement that it believed was existential in its stakes, but was not in any **traditional** sense a war. This expanded the notion of what grand strategy is and which circumstances demand it. The nuclear element of the new grand strategy:

> had no real precedents, beyond the dropping of the two atomic bombs on Japan. And so it focused on finding a new methodology, building scenarios and borrowing from mathematics and probability theory.[96]

The nature of the international system changed in another fundamental way in 1945. Rejecting their previous abandonment of the League of Nations, Americans took primary responsibility for the development of a new international constitutional system that gave a voice to all independent nations and created a mechanism for collective security within the United Nations.[97] Through this means, small nations, many of them coming out from under the yoke of European imperialism, were able to gain forms of influence and leverage never before afforded to them. But, in its ongoing competition with the Soviet Union, the United States also manipulated the politics of smaller nations in order to sustain regimes or produce outcomes favorable to capitalism and hostile to socialism or communism.

The U.S. grand strategy for the Cold War, which went through many iterations between 1945 and 1989, served reasonably well as an overall framework for stability and U.S. influence in the world, even if the Americans sometimes failed to identify their own vital interests, and even if they sometimes alienated nations that did not wish to have to choose between the United States and Soviet models. But the Cold War — fueled by fear and profound mistrust — had its own perverse logic that led to a barely controlled spiral of unprecedentedly lethal arms. The atmosphere of mutually assured destruction was endured not only by the protagonists in the conflict, but also by the entire world. It had a large monetary and psychological cost, and it had an immense set of opportunity costs.[98]

The prevailing tendency to perceive the struggle with the Soviet Union as a zero-sum enterprise, and the domestic political effects this produced, ultimately led the United States into a lengthy ground war in which its own interests were limited, but those of its enemy were unlimited. A desire to reunify and liberate his people after the exit of French colonialists prompted Ho Chi Minh and his followers to fight a fierce people's war against what they perceived to be a series of U.S.-backed puppet governments in Saigon. Unable to build a robust state and effective military around the corrupt regimes in the south, the United States was never able to make adequate headway or extinguish the North Vietnamese will to fight. The fierce irregular fight put up by the North Vietnamese and their supporters in the south was by no means the world's first experience of "people's war" — indeed, Clausewitz and Jomini had been shocked by similar fights (especially the popular Spanish resistance against Napoleon) during their own era. But the Vietnam war surely made clear, once again, the challenge that a great power faces against an enemy willing to fight unconventionally and unremittingly over a protracted period of time.[99] One major result of the war in the United States — the rejection of the draft in favor of an all-volunteer military — would have lasting and transformative consequences for U.S. civil-military relations and U.S. strategy.

In 1989, the rather abrupt collapse of the Soviet Union thrust the United States and its allies into a new security paradigm that was, at first, driven by the self-restructuring of the old Soviet-dominated world and then by the rising threat of al-Qaeda's militant activists. After the latter's attacks on U.S. targets on September 11, 2001, the United States responded by an attack on the Taliban-dominated regime in Afghanistan and then shifted briefly to a preventive war strategy. The latter produced a U.S. war against Iraq in 2003, the goal of which was "regime change" designed to remove Saddam Hussein, whom key American leaders feared might transfer weapons of mass destruction to terrorists. A second but important goal of the war, in the minds of those who commenced it, was to open space for the creation of a new democracy in the Middle East. The project in Iraq was, however, rushed into action without a full analysis of likely consequences. The kind of useful debate that might have taken place was simply absent in a nation traumatized by the shock of a costly and tragic terror attack on its soil. The resulting war, which shifted resources away from the ongoing campaign in Afghanistan and which was mishandled by two different administrations, has seen in its wake a seemingly endless string of disappointments, dashed hopes, and tragedies. The details go far beyond the scope of this monograph, but the war itself, and the U.S. failure to realize its goal of stabilizing Iraq, was a result, in part, of the collapse of a well-functioning civil-military relationship in the United States.[100]

In the second decade of the 21st century, the United States is struggling to contend with the wide array of security threats that compromise its present and its future, including, al-Qaeda, the Islamic State in the Levant, fragile states, international criminal networks, infectious disease, cyberwarfare, and global warming (and the displacement and upheaval the latter is likely to cause). In addition, it faces the challenges posed by the rise of China, a near peer competitor with a large economy and an undemocratic and illiberal system of governance.[101] All this must be managed against the backdrop of dramatically shrinking budgets driven by entitlements to, and medical costs for, an increasingly elderly population. These threats all require strategies that will make intelligent, robust, and defensible linkages between ends sought and limited means available.

THE CHALLENGES OF DEVISING AND IMPLEMENTING STRATEGY AND GRAND STRATEGY

In an article he wrote for *The Washington Post* in December 2009, scholar and former State Department advisor Eliot Cohen explained that, "Strategy is the art of choice that binds means with objectives." He added that it involves "priorities, sequencing, and a theory of victory."[102] The first is terribly important since strategy must involve trade-offs. It requires the practitioner to accept the idea of limited resources, to choose wisely among them, and then to organize and utilize them so that they serve a defined political end. For grand strategy, this demand grows exponentially. One must not only choose wisely among resources, but also integrate, rationalize, and synchronize their use — frequently in conjunction with allies. In fact, Cohen's own experience in government, as an advisor to Secretary of State Condoleezza Rice during the second term of the George W. Bush administration, convinced him that this task is so hard to perform in the maelstrom of day-to-day events that the entire notion of grand strategy might be in doubt. The best one might aim for, instead, is a kind of enlightened and informed muddling through.

In the United States, those who would criticize a given administration's grand strategy for a lack of clarity, purpose, or vision are usually those who are observing it from the outside, often from think tanks and academic posts. Those inside the administration are, instead, frantically busy trying to cope with prevailing events and crises. While they will make efforts to articulate their broad vision in the congressionally mandated *National Security Strategy of the United States* and in speeches at various venues, they will find themselves fighting daily to get out from under the reactive stance that is largely unavoidable inside government and is exacerbated by the battles waged by contending interest groups, the constraints of world and domestic opinion and, most of all, the 24/7 news cycle.

Senior policymakers within the U.S. Government are subjected to hectic schedules that are divided daily into small increments. There is little, if any, time for the kind of reflective thought that allows for a broad perspective or for detailed analysis of any one subject. Robert Jervis has written recently:

> The number of meetings . . . the need to deal with multiple crises simultaneously, the difficulty in getting the relevant information, the growing fatigue, the necessity of dealing with self-important and ill-informed members of Congress . . . and what must be the knowledge that the decisions being made may be misguided take their toll.[103]

Steven Metz has observed that grand strategy "attempts to impose coherence and predictability on an inherently disorderly environment composed of thinking, reacting, competing, and conflicting entities."[104] That coherence must emerge from a domestic interagency process that has its own competitive dynamics and serious challenges of communication flow. Despite their exhausting schedules, all parties who are necessary to the success of a strategy or grand strategy must attempt to stay in ongoing and open communication with one another, not least of all to make sure that the logic relating ends and means is not usurped or undermined by the course of events, or simply forgotten. (Once a problem has existed for any length of time, it often becomes difficult to recall the original logic underpinning the strategy for dealing with it.)

Progress (or lack of it) towards the aim must be monitored, and adjustments must be made in light of setbacks or stagnation. This requirement has significant ramifications at the organizational and bureaucratic levels. In the United States, the National Security Council, as the main interagency coordinating body, has a high responsibility not only to tee up issues appropriately for senior decisionmakers, but also to understand and monitor, to the greatest extent possible, the actions that flow from these decisions. Only in this way can integration and forward momentum be sustained. But the tyranny of immediate events and crises, tight schedules, and complexity of the U.S. interagency system place serious barriers in the path of this ideal.[105]

Political decisionmakers not only must understand when it is justifiable to use military force to solve a political problem, but they must understand the limitations of the instruments that the military wields. They must avoid moving toward violence in the absence of strategy; and they must also understand that violence, once employed, will reshape the political landscape — both domestically and internationally. None of this is easy, and the great contested stew of domestic politics will often complicate their efforts and force their hand. Political decisionmakers must comprehend that the triumphs and failures of the military constantly will redefine which ends are still possible and which ones are not. Finally, they must understand that weariness, emotional fatigue, and shortened attention spans (often caused by the press of events) ineluctably will affect the quality of the choices they make and the policies they implement.

In the United States, few civilians in high policymaking circles have any military experience; they therefore lack a firsthand appreciation of the inherent complexity of military operations, including their propensity for what Clausewitz called "fog" and "friction."[106] Many civilians are inclined to believe that military operations are fairly straightforward, more or less like other business and commercial activities. This, in turn, leads them to be overly optimistic about what missions the military can accomplish and at what cost.[107]

Even academics who study international affairs and strategic studies may be poorly equipped to analyze effectively what Betts calls barriers to effective strategy since, as he explains:

> so few of them anymore learn enough about the processes of decision-making or military operations to grasp how hard it is to implement strategic plans, and few focus on the conversion processes that open gaps between what government leaders decide to do and what governmental organizations implementing those decisions actually *do* do.[108]

In a different but related vein, those on the military side of the civil-military divide often fail to comprehend the overwhelming desire that political decision-makers have for confidence in their choices and their policies. Because they must "sell" their choices to the public, they become ineluctably (and sometimes irrationally) wedded to them: they feel a need to be consistent, to project an image of foresight, wisdom, and determination; and they feel a strong need to uphold the implicit and explicit pact they have made with their own polity. Robert Jervis has explained that:

> For reasons of both psychology and politics, decision makers want to minimize not only actual value trade-offs but also their own perception of them. . . . Maximimizing political support for a policy means arguing that it meets many goals, is supported by many considerations, and has few costs.[109]

Politicians and policymakers are consumed by their own unique challenges and burdens; indeed, they must spend as much time on domestic politics and interagency coordination as they spend on the development of plans. They must, above all, invest an extraordinary amount of time in creating a domestic environment that will enable them to implement, build, and sustain a strategy **in the first place**.[110] Once they invest this time, putting their words and their integrity on the line as they do so, they find that it becomes very hard for them to change course at all, let alone to do so in the timely and adroit way that good strategy often demands.

Because policymakers, especially those closest to the President, want to appear confident in their choices and self-assured as they implement strategic plans, they often resent information from military or intelligence officers that seem to erode that confidence, or present a different opinion. Their response to such cognitive dissonance is often to simply ignore information that does not align with their policy preference or proposed course of action. In other words, the stress inherent in facing the prospect of failure is so crushing that decisionmakers simply avoid it, or at least avoid it for as long as possible.[111]

Just as detailed intelligence can muddy the waters of political decisionmaking (when that information is not wholly supportive of a decision or policy), so too can the military's reflexive conservatism and perceived responsibility to plan for the worst case. This structural tension, which is largely unavoidable, can create serious problems of communication since one side will not want to hear what the other side feels is most important to say. The George W. Bush administration immediately dismissed and discredited Army Chief of Staff Eric Shinseki's estimate of the number of troops that might be required to bring order in Iraq in the aftermath of a war there. Likewise, the Barack Obama administration resented Lieutenant General Stanley McChrystal's estimate of the troop numbers required by a surge in Afghanistan.[112]

Complicating this situation is the fact that politicians will want to respond to crises, most of the time with a limited use of resources. Mimicking the business community, they will want to solve problems in the least amount of time and at the lowest cost. However, the instinctive tendency by democratic politicians to rely on a minimalist approach will place them at odds with military planners who do not wish to risk professional embarrassment due to the under-resourcing of an initiative. Acutely aware that cutting any corner may well mean a real cost in terms of lives, the military prefers to work with a substantial reserve of resources to deploy if things go awry, which, in the realm of conflict and war, they often do.

In situations where American interests are real but limited, and our adversaries interests are unlimited, political leaders often will grasp, first, at a seemingly low-cost option; if it fails, they will face the prospect of doubling down or pulling out—neither of which is appealing. Usually they will select some intermediate option between the two extremes. If compromise is usually a sound instinct for democratic policy-makers, it does not always serve leaders well in this instance since compromises — a middle way between two unhappy options — often prolong conflict without providing the means to end it satisfactorily.[113]

Betts has observed presciently that:

> politicians often conflate strategy with policy objectives (focusing on what the desired outcome should be, simply assuming that force will move the adversary toward it), while soldiers often conflate strategy with operations (focusing on how to destroy targets or defeat enemies tactically, assuming that positive military effects mean positive policy effects).[114]

Policymakers may, indeed, reach too readily for armed force as a preferred instrument because they assume, simplistically, that force will have the desired effect on the enemy, even when those aims cannot possibly be achieved by military arms alone. In the United States, this tendency to reach for the military has been made easier by the creation of a professionalized all-volunteer military and the erosion of the requirement to obtain popular consent, through Congress, for the use of force.[115] For decisionmakers anxious to keep a problem off the front pages, the use of force (including the employment of unmanned aerial vehicles in recent years) can be a seductive option.[116]

The civil-military relationship within a nation is a complex one that is partly structured and partly improvised, but **always** challenging.[117] At no moment in time does it acquire a permanent condition of stability; instead, it must be managed, worked on, and nurtured every single day. A further challenge at the highest levels is that any given administration may attempt to co-opt, politically, the military decisionmakers who work closely with it. An administration may well do this without being aware of it or without fully countenancing how corrosive it is of healthy civil-military relations. Military officers are obliged to give their best professional military advice to civilian decisionmakers. This advice must be as objective as possible and as nonpartisan as possible. But holding on to true objectivity can be challenging, for instance, for a Chairman of the Joint Chiefs of Staff who is the primary military advisor to the President and who works shoulder-to-shoulder with him (or her) in the White House for long periods of time.[118]

Just as military leaders must understand the demands on political decisionmakers, so too must political decisionmakers understand the environment in which military leaders work and the heavy demands and expectations placed upon them. Soldiers (and sailors, marines, and airmen) are unavoidably consumed by the relentless, ever-changing needs of military operations: making and then adapting plans; implementing decisions and revisiting them in light of feedback and data; building necessary infrastructure; supplying and sustaining troops, equipment, morale, and momentum; and keeping all this aligned with the goals and desires of the civilian leadership. Simply the act of getting equipment and personnel to the right place at the right time is an all-consuming task that will supply plenty of its own challenges, setbacks, and moments of high drama. Warfighting is, **in itself**, the most demanding of all human endeavors, not only physically, but also emotionally and intellectually. Indeed, to enter into war is to lift the lid on a Pandora's Box of uncertainty and contingency, with each new act or phase either opening up or closing off future options. It is enough to find ways to fight effectively against an enemy trying to thwart you at every turn. But you must do more: you must tie every military action to the political aims sought by the leaders in charge of the effort. To keep those aims in view and to implement them within the cacophony of a democratic political structure is a challenge of the highest order.[119]

An additional challenge for military leaders, which civilians would do well to understand, is the lure or the appeal of operations. These possess a hard-to-resist attraction, not only because they are demanding and thus time-consuming, but also because they represent the place where military officers can demonstrate the full complement of skills that their long institutional training and education have bestowed upon them. It is in this realm where they are most comfortable and where they feel they can make the most difference, both professionally and personally. Strachan has pointed out that armed forces are inherently attracted to the operational level of war: "it allows them to appropriate what they see as the acme of their professional competence, separate from the trammels and constraints of political and policymaking direction."[120] Mackubin Thomas Owens has observed that "wartime service doctrines will dominate the conduct of operations if strategy is absent."[121]

Just as civilian decisionmakers will feel pressure to stay the course once a decision is made, so too will military planners once they have embarked on a campaign—even if it was not in line, originally, with their own preferences or advice. This is so because once an operation is underway, it places the military's professional expertise and competence under a national spotlight. Like all institutions, they want to perform well when they are called upon to do so. They want to justify their existence, avoid embarrassment, and justify the sizable expenditures on equipment, resources, and education they argued for and gained through testimony to Congress and the American people. Their own strong arguments for a campaign plan or piece of kit can lock them into a set of expectations they wish to see realized.[122] Even more importantly, the military will seek to carry a campaign through to success to justify the human losses sustained in the midst of it. These losses are felt keenly, and they fuel determination to stay the course and uphold the cause for which brothers- and sisters-in-arms have given their lives.

All this necessarily creates bias in the way that the military reads metrics and attempts to assess progress in an operation, campaign, or war that is underway. This is exacerbated by a "can do" culture that will be inclined to dismiss or downplay evidence indicating that a military mission is failing to meet its objectives. In his memoir about his time spent as Secretary of Defense, Robert Gates wrote: "'The more time you spend in Afghanistan,' I told the President, 'the closer to the front you get, the more optimistic people are'."[123] Both civilian and military leaders have strong psychological incentives to filter information and to deny — or simply screen out — information suggesting that their current course of action is problematic. Acknowledging failure (or simply a lack of progress) and then adapting involves considerable psychological stress, and frequently, a great deal of pain.[124]

Yet another structural barrier to effective communication between civil and military leaders stems, again, from the nature of the division itself — a division that exists in democracies for sound and admirable reasons. In a representative democracy, elected civilians are the ones who quite rightly have the responsibility for consequential choices affecting the polity as a whole. If their choices prove misguided or simply unpopular, elected civilians can be removed in the next voting cycle. Since no one elects military officers and they are not, therefore, subject to sanction at the ballot box, they ought not hold the lion's share of influence over national decisions about the start of a war, the political aims of a war, or the ending of a war. But how does a military leader confine himself (or herself) to offering professional military advice when any use of force — and certainly any entry into war — has so many political dimensions? If we accept the Clausewitzian notion that war is a continuation of politics by other means, is not the military planner necessarily thrust into the realm of politics, whether he or she wants to be there or not? This is an important question that is not discussed often enough in the realm of professional military education. In his memoir, McChrystal observed that, during his service in Afghanistan, "The process of formulating, negotiating, articulating, and then prosecuting even a largely military campaign involved politics at multiple levels that were impossible to ignore."[125]

A fear of getting ahead of the President, or getting crosswise with the White House in general, is something that most high-level military officers take **very** seriously; they know that it can have profoundly negative consequences for the nation, not to mention the consequences for their own careers and reputations. Most, therefore, will tread quite carefully when they walk the line, perhaps "high wire" is the better phrase, that runs between political choices and military ones. U.S. Presidents are highly sensitive to the history of military interference in politics; indeed, General Douglas MacArthur's insubordination during the Harry Truman presidency left a stain that lingers to this day and haunts contemporary civil-military relations.[126]

The trust that is so essential to sound civil-military decisionmaking must be built, in part, on education, and on the belief that generals will not use their power and influence to meddle in the realm of democratic politics.[127] If military leaders leak information about national strategy (in order to influence the direction or momentum of a debate), the result can be highly corrosive, causing subsequent communication to become constrained and fraught. Similar outcomes result if civilians believe that military leaders are trying to game, stack, or stall a consequential decision.

Wary of all this, and aware of the way that military influence can and does continue to upend democratic governance around the world, most officers try to leave themselves a safety zone designed to buffer them from charges of political behavior or political interference. But discerning exactly where that safety zone begins and ends can be highly stressful. Even officers who are trying to be very careful can find themselves wandering into dangerous territory. On the other hand, military leaders simply may not foresee all the political and strategic consequences that will flow from what they believe to be an operational (or even tactical) decision. Perhaps the most stunning example of this oversight was Admiral Isoroku Yamamoto's decision not to share plans about the Pearl Harbor attack with key civilians because he felt that the attack plan was about military operations and tactics rather than strategy.[128]

All this complicates the ability (and, indeed, willingness) of senior-level military officers to engage in realms that appear to be within the lane of other authorities or agencies, including the State Department or the United States Agency for International Development. But regardless of their concerns, and in the interest of sound strategy, they must be prepared to work together with civilian authorities to figure out how to walk the civil-military high wire successfully. By no means does this imperative end at the moment of an armistice. Since winning a war means finding a way to create a satisfactory and sustainable peace, military officers must be willing to learn, embrace, and utilize a range of tools in the transition from combat operations to stability and peacekeeping. Even if other agencies of the government own large swaths of the expertise in this realm, the military will own the manpower and the equipment required for the implementation of goals and the guarantee of satisfactory outcomes. It will be necessary for military leaders to stay involved in planning and to be prepared to employ the threat and/or use of force as coercive leverage if such leverage proves necessary to produce and sustain acceptable political outcomes.[129]

At all levels, officers must be willing and able to see and understand the political, cultural, historical, and social contexts that shape the foreign environment in which they are operating. A failure to do this (along with a narrow focus on the strictly military aspects of an operation), in nearly every case, will prohibit them from realizing the results they seek.[130] This holds not only for campaigns, but also for training and advising missions. If, for instance, U.S. troops make heroic efforts to train foreign troops in marksmanship, leadership, and tactics without recognizing that the environment those foreign troops operate in is dominated by corruption and graft, their investment of time and energy is likely to be for naught.

In counterinsurgency (COIN) operations, planners must pay particular attention to the political environment since bad governance (which was the root of the problem to begin with) will make impossible or obviate any serious gains on the battlefield. Explaining that COIN can be successful in many circumstances, Stephen Biddle warns that hard-won gains can be quickly lost:

> COIN is obviously hard and slow. But the Afghan experience shows that current U.S. methods can return threatened districts to government control, when conducted with the necessary time and resources. This certainly does require combat and hard fighting. Counterinsurgency is not social work, and its purpose is not to make local civilians like Americans.

Importantly, though, he adds: "But combat and security alone will have difficulty sustaining control if all they do is allow a predatory government to exploit the population for the benefit of unrepresentative elites."[131]

Stove-piping information, institutional infighting, and organizational and cultural biases can cause the strategy process to founder on the shoals of ignorance, self-interest, or arrogance. But if we are intentional about recognizing these phenomena, we can work to ameliorate their effects. Even though there are permanent, unavoidable bureaucratic and civil-military tensions that complicate the articulation and execution of strategy, it is possible—through education and action—to shift the odds in favor of success. Interpersonal relationships will matter, too, especially at the highest levels; key players must be willing and able to pull towards an agreed-upon end state. If they refuse, even the most robust strategy will be in jeopardy.

Are Better Outcomes Possible?

Peter Layton has identified two alternatives to grand strategy that may be valid for some actors under certain circumstances. "Opportunism" posits that actors may change, shift, or evolve in order to take advantage of possibilities as they present themselves. This requires not so much a specific aim point, or end, than a general direction. It is an option for actors who may not have the resources to shape outcomes, but instead may wish to grasp and exploit the breaks that come their way. It surely has advantages, not least being that it can be far less resource-demanding than grand strategy. But it has downsides, too. It is reactive, leaving an actor largely at the mercy of outside forces it cannot control: "the state using opportunism does not initiate and therefore must accept boundaries determined elsewhere; the state is part of another's project and is responsive to that."[132]

The flip side of the opportunism coin is risk management. Layton explains that in this approach, an actor will seek mainly to avoid harm to itself as a result of the forces around it. Actors can anticipate potential harm and take steps to make themselves less directly or acutely subject to it. These steps can include "building capabilities and capacities to survive shocks," or "continuing operation[s] in the presence of external stresses," or "absorbing shocks and evolving in response." These might be political and/or physical in nature.[133] An example of the latter might include the building of protective walls to hold back rising seas caused by melting Arctic ice. Like opportunism, though, risk management will not offer the sense of agency that strategy and grand strategy can confer when they are well-designed and implemented.

Strategy always will demand clear and honest interaction and cooperation between two very distinct tribes, civilian and military, who have different priorities, cultures, and modes of operating. At the end of the day, neither structural tensions nor inherent problems of communication and implementation should prohibit strategic decisionmakers from **striving towards** an ideal and working to make their choices as intelligent and informed as possible.[134] Indeed, this is a moral imperative whenever lives are on the line.

Because of the myriad opportunities for miscommunication and failure, resilience and recovery mechanisms must be built into the strategy process. These mechanisms depend above all on healthy, trust-based organizations (and relationships) that facilitate learning and adapting—both from the top down and from the bottom up. The learning and adapting depend, of course, on analysis and critical thinking. Being able to ask the right questions at the right time is key—but this skill requires moral courage, sound judgment, and wisdom on both the civilian and military sides of the aisle. Hard questioning, analytical thinking, and the repeated challenging of assumptions are requirements of strategy, especially in wartime. This skill can be honed in many ways, but among the most important is the use of historical case studies in strategic education. These are important for both civilian and military pedagogy. Case studies allow students to go beyond frameworks and definitions; they invite students to plunge into the details of the strategy making process, illuminating where challenges, frictions, and potential miscommunications are to be found.

History and historical case studies are vital to the development of critical thinking skills. To attempt to explain the past in a coherent way is to wrestle with evidence and argument. We seek out arguments with the greatest explanatory power, and the search sharpens our critical faculties and forces us to use our logical and analytical powers to their maximum capacity. Explaining the past also forces us to prioritize and systematize the information available to us: a useful explanation of the past has to be more than a jumble of undifferentiated facts; instead it must be a rational, robust, coherent argument that rests on evidence from the record and is not easily dismissed or replaced by another argument. To study history is to bring discipline to our minds. One noted scholar has explained that history trains students:

> in the rules of evidence and logic, teaches them how to approximate truth through the patient exposure of falsehood, and gives them the mental trellis they need to place themselves in time and space and organize every other sort of knowledge they acquire in the humanities and sciences.[135]

Of course, history never repeats itself exactly, but the study of history can help us learn to see patterns and trends more clearly. Once we understand the patterns of the past, we can learn what kinds of questions are most useful to ask ourselves about the present. While these questions will not provide us with immunity from mistakes or protect us from false analogies, they may well help us to become more self-aware and more alert to our own circumstances. They may help us develop the quality of empathy, which is such a central part of emotional intelligence and successful analysis.[136]

Civilian students of strategy ought to be given opportunities to immerse themselves, occasionally, in the culture of the military in order to learn its vocabulary, its priorities, and its principles of functioning and organizing.[137] Military students should have opportunities, if they so desire, to study for periods of time in civilian academies or to rotate for periods of time into civilian institutions. Nonmilitary members of the interagency ought to be encouraged to study, side-by-side with military officers, in senior staff colleges. Such activities can aid in producing multilingual individuals who understand both civilian and military cultures and language and therefore can act as interlocutors and translators between the two groups. In addition, those who have acquired such abilities through long service in the Washington arena should perceive themselves as crucial bridge-builders in the strategy process.[138]

Military students in particular ought to have every opportunity to learn to see their world through lenses other than their own. Cultural awareness and cultural literacy are essential to politics and to strategy, and thus military decisionmakers, in addition to political decisionmakers, must be adroit in these realms. One way in which this need has been addressed in recent years has been through the increased numbers of international students coming to U.S. staff colleges and learning alongside their American counterparts. If the former gain useful knowledge to take home with them, they also provide key bodies of knowledge — and essential forms of cultural awareness — to their American brothers- and sisters-in-arms.

Even if civilian policymakers inevitably are trapped by the high volume of information and the rapid demand for decisions in the age of the Internet and the 24-hour news cycle, they can try to educate themselves in order to prepare for this situation. Occasional table-top exercises and red-teaming of thorny problems are likely to prove worthwhile—not least because they facilitate the building of personal relationships and allow necessary forms of civil-military communication to be practiced. Time invested in them, especially early on in the life of an administration, is likely to pay major dividends later. In 2006, Michele Flournoy and Shawn Brimley looked to the Dwight Eisenhower administration's "Project Solarium" for a way to imagine a major reanalysis of U.S. *National Security Strategy* for the 21st century. In the summer of 1953, Solarium brought together key national security professionals, insisting that they pose deep questions that would force a close look at the structural underpinnings of the existing strategy for waging the Cold War. It was a model of its kind and, indeed, should serve as a template for future efforts of a similar type.[139]

On the military side, skilled, efficient, and highly competent staff work is essential; there is simply no substitute for it. Finding answers to essential questions will depend on the presence of a skilled and diligent staff of dedicated professionals who are well-informed, instinctively analytical, and adaptive. They must be willing to allow information to flow freely, even from the bottom up; and they must be open to information and advice from partners and from subject matter experts. Neither strategy nor grand strategy can rest upon individual genius (although good fortune can sometimes lend a hand). Some of those we frequently identify as successful strategists, including George Marshall and Churchill, promulgated seriously flawed strategies at various points in their careers. But they had people alongside them who could offer contrary opinions and catch errors; and they had organizations under them that could do dedicated, first-rate staff work, the kind of work that allows for learning, adaption, and adjustment.[140] Indeed, adroit-ness, perhaps, is the single most important quality of strategy — the quality that is most likely to give an actor an advantage over an adversary.

To be even partially successful, a strategy must have staying power, resiliency, and robustness. All parties must realize this and commit to it, even when domestic political interest has begun to wane and new items creep onto the security agenda. With reference to the military instrument, Betts has observed:

> If effective military strategy is to be real rather than illusory, one must be able to devise a rational scheme to achieve an objective through combat or the threat of it; implement the scheme with forces; keep the plan working in the face of enemy reactions (which should be anticipated in the plan); and achieve something close to the objective.[141]

This is surely a nontrivial set of demands, but it is fully justified, he argued, in situations where the stakes are high, lives are at risk, and failure will be costly on multiple levels.

Historian Walter McDougall has defined sound grand strategy as "an equation of ends and means so sturdy that it triumphs despite serial setbacks at the level of strategy, operations, and campaigns. The classic example is Allied grand strategy during World War II."[142] Serial setbacks surely beset U.S. grand strategy in World War II, from the fall of the Philippines to the missteps at the Kasserine Pass in Tunisia; from the chaos of the Sicily landing to the early failures of the strategic bombing offensive; from the glider disasters at Normandy and the torpedo failures in the Pacific to the enemy counterpunches at Arnhem, The Nether-lands, and the Battle of the Bulge in the Ardennes, Belgium. But each time, the Americans, in concert with their allies, recovered and adjusted.

Finally, all parties must embrace the idea that the use of force must always be a last resort. While it can and should work constantly in the background as a form of potential leverage and coercion, it should be wielded only sparingly and soberly, when other options fail. In any situation where lives are at stake, we have a powerful moral obligation to proceed carefully and with restraint, and to craft strategy and grand strategy that is as sound, efficient, and adaptive as possible.[143] Because it is so challenging on so many levels, strategy is difficult to practice in any idealized form. But it is not an impossible art. Diligent students of strategy who are fully alive to its complexities and demands will be prepared to anticipate and accommodate the inevitable twists and turns, setbacks, and disappointments they will face — and will be asked to overcome.

ENDNOTES

1. Beatrice Heuser, *The Evolution of Strategy*, Cambridge, UK: Cambridge University Press, 2010, p. 4; Antulio Echevarria, *Reconsidering the American Way of War*, Washington, DC: Georgetown University Press, 2014, p. 47; Hew Strachen, *The Direction of War: Contemporary Strategy in Historical Perspective*, Cambridge, UK: Cambridge University Press, 2013, p. 28.

2. In reference to this problem, Strachan has opined that, "The word strategy has acquired a universality which has robbed it of meaning, and left it only with banalities." See Hew Strachen, *The Direction of War*, p. 27; also see Lawrence Freedman, *Strategy: A History*, New York: Oxford University Press, 2013, p. x; Hal Brands, *What Good is Grand Strategy?* Ithaca, NY: Cornell University Press, 2014, p. 3.

3. See, for instance, Barry Posen and Andrew Ross, "Competing Visions for U.S. Grand Strategy," *International Security*, Vol. 21, No. 3, 1997, pp. 5-53; Elbridge Colby, "Grand Strategy: Contending Contemporary Analyst Views and Implications for the U.S. Navy," CRM D0025423.A2, Arlington, VA: Center for Naval Analysis, November 2011.

4. For important insights, see Richard K. Betts, "Is Strategy an Illusion?" *International Security*, Vol. 25, No. 2, Fall 2000, pp. 5-50; and Richard K. Betts, *American Force: Dangers, Delusions and Dilemmas in National Security*, New York: Columbia University Press, 2012.

5. On this point, students of strategy have much to learn from students of cognitive psychology who investigate how we absorb and process information through our senses. Contemporary political scientists have helped us learn to apply cognitive psychology to the behavior of decisionmakers charged with strategic choices. For the foundational literature, see Robert Jervis, *Perception and Misperception in International Politics*, Princeton, NJ: Princeton University Press, 1976; Robert Axelrod, *Framework for a General Theory of Cognition and Choice*, Berkeley, CA: Institute of International Studies, 1972; Irving L. Janis and Leon Mann, *Decision Making: A Psychological Analysis of Conflict, Choice, and Commitment*, New York: Free Press, 1977. For a recent application of some of the insights from this literature, see an illuminating essay by Robert Jervis, "Why Intelligence and Policymakers Clash," *Political Science Quarterly*, Vol. 125, No. 2, Summer 2010, especially pp. 197-200.

6. The relationship between the leader and the military institution(s) within a state (or nonstate actor) can greatly affect the behavior and potential competence of the military within that state. This ought to be factored into strategic analysis. For insights, see Stephen Biddle and Robert Zirkle, "Technology, Civil-Military Relations, and Warfare in the Developing World," *Journal of Strategic Studies*, Vol. 19, No. 2, 1996, pp. 171-212; Stephen Biddle, "Victory Misunderstood: What the Gulf War Tells Us about the Future of Conflict," *International Security*, Vol. 21, No. 2, Autumn 1996, pp. 139-179.

7. Sir Michael Howard has identified four "forgotten dimensions" of strategy: operational, logistical, social, and technologi-

cal. Colin Gray has identified a much longer list of elements to be considered. He divided these into three sub-categories: people and politics; preparation for war; and war proper. See Sir Michael Howard, "The Forgotten Dimensions of Strategy," *Foreign Affairs*, Vol. 57, No. 5, Summer 1979; also see Colin Gray, *Modern Strategy*, New York: Oxford University Press, 1999, pp. 23-44. Edward Luttwak describes strategy as a "multilevel edificace." See Edward Luttwak, *Strategy: The Logic of War and Peace*, Rev. Ed., Cambridge, MA: Harvard University Press, 2001, especially p. 209. For a brief but perceptive examination of some failed strategies of the past, see Paul Kennedy, "Grand Strategies and Less Than Grand Strategies: A Twentieth Century Critique," in Lawrence Freedman, Paul Hayes, and Robert O'Neill, eds., *War Strategy and International Politics: Essays in Honour of Sir Michael Howard*, Oxford, UK: Clarendon, 1992, pp. 227-242.

8. For a perceptive analysis of these challenges, see Betts, *American Force*, pp. 232-271. See also Williamson Murray, Richard Hart Sinnreich, and James Lacey, eds., *The Shaping of Grand Strategy: Policy Diplomacy and War*, New York: Cambridge University Press, 2011, p. 254.

9. See Paul Kennedy, ed., *Grand Strategies in War and Peace*, New Haven: Yale University Press, 1991, p. 6.

10. For a useful overview, see Stephen Biddle, "Strategy in War," PSonline, *www.apsanet.org,* July 2007.

11. Biddle, "Strategy in War." Strachan has insisted that the more limited, short-term quality of "military strategy" must not be substituted, one for one, with the broader, longer-term orientation of "grand strategy." He argues, "By using the same word, 'strategy,' in both sets of circumstances, we create an expectation, each of the other, which neither can properly fulfill." See Hew Strachan, "Strategy and Contingency," *International Affairs*, Vol. 87, No. 6, 2011, p. 1281. He points out that what the United States calls "grand strategy" is called 'national strategy' in many other nations of the world.

12. John Lewis Gaddis, "What is Grand Strategy?" Karl Von Der Heyden Distinguished Lecture, Duke University, Durham, NC, February 26, 2009, keynote address for the conference,

"American Grand Strategy after War," p. 7, available from *tiss-nc.org/wp-content/uploads/2015/01/KEYNOTE.Gaddis50thAniv2009.pdf*. Brands echoed this idea a few years later, stating, "grand strategy involves figuring out how to align today's initiatives with tomorrow's desired end state—how to get from where one is to where one ultimately wants to go." Brands, p. 4. For a description of some definitions as they were developed at a recent conference on strategy held by the U.S. Army, see John C. Valledor, "Strategy Education across the Professional Military Education Enterprise," *Parameters*, May 18, 2015, available from *www.strategicstudies institute.army.mil/index.cfm/articles/Strategy-Education/2015/05/18*.

13. Samuel Eliot Morison, *Strategy and Compromise*, Boston, MA: Little Brown, 1958, pp. 4-5.

14. These include the Naval War College, the Air War College, the U.S. Army War College, and the National War College.

15. For detailed descriptions of what is meant by the senior staff colleges when they use the terms "ends, ways, and means," see Harry R. Yarger, "Toward a Theory of Strategy: Art Lykke and the Army War College Strategy Model" in James Bartholomees, ed., *U.S. Army War College Guide to National Security Policy and Strategy*, 2nd Ed., June 2006, pp. 111-112; and Harry R. Yarger, *Strategic Theory for the 21st Century: The Little Book on Big Strategy*, Carlisle, PA: Strategic Studies Institute, U.S. Army War College, February 2006. Mackubin Thomas Owens has explained the relationship concisely: "strategy describes the way in which the available means will be employed to achieve the ends of policy." See Mackubin Thomas Owens, "Strategy and the Strategic Way of Thinking," *Naval War College Review*, Autumn 2007, pp. 111-124.

16. Linda Robinson, Paul D. Miller, John Gordon IV, Jeffrey Decker, Michael Schwille, and Raphael S. Cohen, *Improving Strategic Competence: Lessons from 13 Years of War*, Arlington, VA: RAND Arroyo Center, 2014, p. xiii, available from *www.rand.org/content/dam/rand/pubs/research_reports/RR800/RR816/RAND_RR816.pdf*; See also Valledor.

17. Robinson *et al.*, p. xiii.

18. In his classic work on civil-military relations, Samuel Huntington argued for a system of "objective control," enabling civilians to control the military by carefully delineating the political and military spheres and keeping them as distinct as possible. Civilians would retain dominance in the political realm, while handing authority to the military in its own sphere of professional expertise. Through this bargain, the United States could simultaneously protect itself from external threats while guarding against military meddling in the political realm. Huntington felt this was the best way to locate a competent, capable military inside a liberal democratic system of governance. See Samuel Huntington, *The Soldier and the State*, Cambridge, MA: Harvard University Press, 1957; Samuel Huntington, "Civilian Control and the Constitution," *American Political Science Review*, Vol. 50, No. 3, September 1956, pp. 676-699. The literature that has followed in the wake of this argument—both supporting and critiquing it—is vast.

19. In the latter portions of this monograph, I explore the political terrain that military officers need to understand; equally, I explore some of the military fundamentals that civilians need to understand.

20. In an important essay addressing key aspects of this issue, Richard Betts has written:

> One could make the case that for ideal integration of objectives, strategy, and operations, civilians and military should be equally conversant in each others' terms of reference and should participate equally at all stages. In the end, however, few would deny that there is some level of high politics at which soldiers should be silent, and some level of tactical specificity or micromanagement where civilians should keep their hands off.

He adds, "Equality in strategic discussion does not compromise the civilians' ultimate primacy. Presidents have the right to be wrong in the end, but generals should have every chance to prevent error before that end." Richard K. Betts, "Are Civil-Military Relations Still a Problem?" in Suzanne Nielsen and Don M. Snider, eds., *American Civil-Military Relations: The Soldier and the State in a New Era*, Baltimore, MD: Johns Hopkins University Press, 2009, pp. 11-41. For quoted material, see pp. 36, 40.

21. Robinson *et al*, pp. 47-48; Janine Davidson, "The Contemporary Presidency: Civil-Military Friction and Presidential Decision Making: Explaining the Broken Dialogue," *Presidential Studies Quarterly*, Vol. 43, No. 1, 2013, p. 141. While some of his arguments are controversial, one might also consult Dayne E. Nix, "American Civil-Military Relations: Samuel Huntington and the Political Dimensions of Military Professionalism," *The Naval War College Review*, Vol. 65, No. 2, Spring 2012, pp. 88-104.

22. Betts, "Is Strategy an Illusion?" p. 7. For some insights into the reasons for inadequacy on the civilian side, see Tami Davis Biddle and Robert M. Citino, "The Role of Military History in the Contemporary Academy," a Society for Military History (SMH) White Paper available on the SMH website; reprinted in the February 2015 edition of *Footnotes*, the online journal of the Foreign Policy Research Institute and in *Army History*, No. 26, Summer 2015, pp. 24-30.

23. Yale's Grand Strategy Program and the programs of Columbia's Saltzman Institute for War and Peace Studies (including prominently, its Summer Workshop on the Analysis of Military Strategy and Operations) have made admirable efforts to help bridge this civil-military divide. In recent years, Duke University has developed a strong program in grand strategy. Other notable programs that cover elements of this important topic include: those at the School of Advanced International Studies at Johns Hopkins University; MIT; Temple University; the Ohio State University; George Washington University; the University of Texas; Dartmouth University; Georgetown University; and, Texas A&M University.

24. Mackubin Thomas Owens has written: "In general, strategy provides a conceptual link between national ends and scarce resources, both the transformation of those resources into means during peacetime and the application of those means during war." See Owens, "Strategy and the Strategic Way of Thinking," p. 112.

25. See Thomas Mahnken, ed. *Competitive Strategies for the 21st Century: Theory, History, and Practice*, Stanford, CA: Stanford Unversity Press, 2012.

26. Sir Michael Howard, "Grand Strategy in the Twentieth Century," *Defence Studies*, Vol. 1, No. 1, September 2010, pp. 1-10, especially p. 6.

27. For perceptive insights, see David Edgerton, *Britain's War Machine: Weapons, Resources, and Experts in the Second World War*, Oxford, UK: Oxford University Press, 2011; and Paul Kennedy, *Engineers of Victory: The Problem Solvers Who Turned the Tide in the Second World War*, New York: Random House, 2013.

28. For a sophisticated overview, see G. John Ikenberry, *After Victory: Institutions, Strategic Restraint, and the Rebuilding of Order after Major Wars*, Princeton, NJ: Princeton University Press, 2001; and *Liberal Leviathan: The Origins, Crisis, and Transformation of the American World Order*, Princeton, NJ: Princeton University Press, 2011. This U.S. dominated system has surely not been without its critics. For an insightful treatment of its origins, see Adam Tooze, *The Deluge: The Great War, America and the Remaking of the Global Order, 1916-1931*, London, UK: Allen Lane, 2014.

29. Charles Hill has written: "Aristotle would use the Iliad to teach the first principle of statecraft: diplomacy and power are indispensable and must be used, for best effect, in tandem." See Charles Hill, *Grand Strategies: Literature, Statecraft, and World Order*, New Haven, CT: Yale University Press, 2010, p. 9.

30. Betts, "Is Strategy an Illusion?" pp. 5-50. Quoted material on p. 5.

31. John Lewis Gaddis, "The Rise, Fall and Future of Deterrence," *Foreign Affairs*, Winter 1983/84. See also Peter Layton, "The Idea of Grand Strategy," *The RUSI* (Royal United Services Institute) *Journal*, Vol. 157, No. 4, online, August 15, 2012, pp. 56-61, especially pp. 57-58; Owens, "Strategy and the Strategic Way of Thinking," p. 111.

32. Colin Gray, *The Strategy Bridge, Theory for Practice*, New York: Oxford University Press, 2011, p. 3.

33. Layton, "The Idea of Grand Strategy," p. 58. He adds that grand strategy also concerns itself with "assembling the manpower, money and material necessary to build and sustain the means needed."

34. Under the heading of resources, he included economic, technological, and scientific resources; diplomacy; and national morale and political culture. See Kennedy, ed., *Grand Strategies in War and Peace*, pp. 4-5. Brands adds that "a grand strategy represents and integrated scheme of interests, threats, resources, and policies." Brands, p. 3.

35. Betts, "Is Strategy an Illusion?" p. 6. He notes, "The logic at each level is supposed to govern the one below and serve the one above."

36. Writing about strategy involving military operations, Betts observes that:

> Strategy fails when some link in the planned chain of cause and effect from low-level tactics to high-level political outcomes is broken, when military objectives come to be pursued for their own sake without reference to their political effect, or when policy initiatives depend on military operations that are infeasible.

Betts, "Is Strategy an Illusion?" p. 7.

37. See Yarger, "Toward a Theory of Strategy," p. 112. F. G. Hoffman has written about the constraints on strategy. See F. G. Hoffman, "Grand Strategy: The Fundamental Considerations," *Orbis*, Fall 2014, pp. 472-485.

38. Strachan, "Strategy and Contingency," p. 1281.

39. Carl von Clausewitz, *On War*, Michael Howard and Peter Paret, eds. and trans., Princeton, NJ: Princeton University Press, 1976, pp. 119-121. See also Antulio Echevarria, *Clausewitz and Contemporary War*, Oxford, MA: Oxford University Press, 2007, especially pp. 103-109.

40. There are many worthwhile overviews of British strategy in World War II. See Williamson Murray, "British Military Effectiveness in the Second World War," in Williamson Murray and Allan Millett, eds., *Military Effectiveness*, Vol. III, Boston, MA: Unwin Hyman, 1988, pp. 90-135. A recent treatment is David French, "British Military Strategy" (and the related bibliographical essay),

in John Ferris and Evan Mawdsley, eds., *The Cambridge History of the Second World War*, Vol. I, Cambridge, UK: Cambridge University Press, 2015, pp. 28-50, 716-718.

41. B. H. Liddell Hart, *Strategy*, 2nd Rev. Ed., London, UK: Faber and Faber, 1967, p. 322. The book's first edition appeared in 1954.

42. Morison, p. 6. He stated: "grand strategy or higher strategy is simply national foreign policy continued in time of war."

43. Edward Meade Earle, ed., *Makers of Modern Strategy*, Princeton, NJ: Princeton University Press, 1943, p. viii.

44. Liddell Hart, quoted in Morison, p. 6.

45. It is important to realize that, for a peace to be stable over time, former rivals **will need to agree** that the resulting situation is in some sense "better" than it was before. Liddell Hart realizes that "winning the peace" can be a complex and demanding process. I find this concept useful even though I do not prefer to use the phrase "winning the peace." Rather, I see warfighting (or the phrase "fighting and winning the nation's wars") as **inclusive of** the attainment of the peace. In other words, warfighting **includes** war termination. Violence merely opens the space for the vital political work that can flow from it. As Clausewitz understood, war is a continuation of politics; political bargaining carried on through violence reveals further information about the way that rivals perceive stakes, undertake commitment, and sustain will. Once those have been revealed, a new equilibrium becomes possible. See, in general, Thomas Schelling's seminal volume, *Arms and Influence*, New Haven, CT: Yale University Press, 1966. Also see Nadia Schadlow,"War and the Art of Governance," *Parameters*, Vol. 33, No. 3, 2003, pp. 85–94; Nadia Schadlow and Richard Lacquement, "Winning Wars, not Just Battles: Expanding the Military Profession to Incorporate Stability Operations," in Nielsen and Snider, eds., *American Civil-Military Relations: The Soldier and the State in a New Era*, pp. 112-132.

46. For a perceptive insight, see H. R. McMaster, "The Pipe Dream of Easy War," *The New York Times*, July 20, 2013, available from *www.nytimes.com/2013/07/21/opinion/sunday/the-pipe-dream-of-easy-war.html?pagewanted=all&_r=0*.

47. Howard, "Grand Strategy in the Twentieth Century," p. 4. He echoes A. J. P. Taylor's claim in *The Struggle for Mastery in Europe, 1848-1918*, Oxford, UK: Oxford University Press, 1954, p. 528.

48. This idea, which gained traction during the Eisenhower administration, argued that if one nation fell to communism, it would affect those around it, in the same way that a falling domino knocks over those around it. See, for instance, Frederik Logevall, *Choosing War: The Lost Chance for Peace and the Escalation of War in Vietnam*, Berkeley, CA: University of California Press, 1999, p. 31.

49. See generally Frederick Logevall, *Embers of War: The Fall of an Empire and the Making of America's Vietnam*, New York: Random House, 2013; also see Doris Kearns, *Lyndon Johnson and The American Dream*, New York: Harper and Row, 1976, pp. 263-265.

50. Bernard Brodie, *War and Politics*, London, UK: Cassell, 1973, pp. 2, 343-345.

51. This problem surely beset Britain and the United States in the last months of 1944 and the early months of 1945, when fissures in the Anglo-American "special relationship" became heated, emotional, and public. See, for instance, Max Hastings, *Winston's War: Churchill, 1940-1945*, New York: Knopf, 2010, pp. 422-449.

52. Antulio Echevarria, "After Afghanistan: Lessons for NATO's Future Wars," *RUSI Journal*, Vol. 159, No. 3, July 2014, pp. 20-23.

53. Schadlow, "War and the Art of Governance"; H. R. McMaster, "Decentralization vs Centralization," in Thomas Donnelly and Frederick W. Kagan, *Lessons for a Long War: How America Can Win on New Battlefields*, Washington, DC: American Enterprise Institute, 2010; Nix, "American Civil-Military Relations," pp. 99-101. William Flavin, "Planning for Conflict Termination and Post-Conflict Success," *Parameters,* Autumn 2003, pp. 95-112, available from *strategicstudiesinstitute.army.mil/pubs/parameters/Articles/03autumn/flavin.pdf.* On war termination generally, see Gideon Rose, *How Wars End*, New York: Simon and Schuster,

2010; and Matthew Moten, ed., *Between War and Peace*, New York: Free Press, 2011.

54. For reasons to approach the phrase "strategic culture" with care, see Antulio Echevarria, "American Strategic Culture: Problems and Prospects," in Hew Strachan and Sibylle Scheipers, *The Changing Character of War*, Oxford, UK: Oxford University Press, 2011, pp. 431-445. For interpretations of the phrase, see Theo Farrell, "Strategic Culture and American Empire," *SAIS* [School of Advanced and International Studies] *Review*, Vol. 25, No. 2, Summer-Fall 2005, pp. 3-18; and Thomas Mahnken, *United States Strategic Culture*, Ft. Belvoir, VA: Defense Threat Reduction Agency, Science Applications International Corporation, 2006. More generally, see Wayne Lee, *Warfare and Culture in World History*, New York: New York University Press, 2011.

55. For a concise introduction to this topic, see Mackubin Thomas Owens, *US Civil-Military Relations After 9/11: Renegotiating the Civil-Military Bargain*, New York: Continuum, 2011, pp. 12-43. For interesting insights into the 19th century debate over civil-military relations in wartime, see John Shy, "Jomini," in Peter Paret, ed., *Makers of Modern Strategy from Machiavelli to the Nuclear Age*, Princeton, NJ: Princeton University Press, 1986, pp. 160-162.

56. Strachan, *The Direction of War*, p. 28.

57. For an illuminating yet succinct foray into this topic, see Donald Kagan, "Athenian Strategy in the Peloponnesian War" in Williamson Murray, MacGregor Knox, and Alvin Bernstein, eds., *The Making of Strategy: Rulers, States, and War*, Cambridge, UK: Cambridge University Press, 1994, pp. 24-55. Scholars wishing to go deeper will want to examine more of Kagan's extraordinary body of work.

58. Equally, we can identify elements of strategy in the planning and implementation of action by other commanders who led armies during the Peloponnesian War, including Bracidas, Alcibiades, and Nicias. See the seminal history of the war (written by Thucydides and captured in many modern, English language editions); among the best of these is *The Landmark Thucydides*, Robert Strassler, ed., New York, Free Press, 1996.

59. The two most highly regarded translations are Samuel B. Griffith, *Sun Tzu The Art of War*, New York: Oxford University Press, 1963; and Ralph Sawyer, *Sun Tzu The Art of War*, Boulder, CO: Westview Press, 1994.

60. For its armies, Rome also drew upon two outside groups: the Latins who were linguistically similar to the Romans, and the non-Latin tribes in Italy who were subject to Rome's will. See Alvin Bernstein, "The Strategy of a Warrior-State: Rome and the Wars against Carthage, 264-201 BC," in Murray, Knox, and Bernstein, eds., pp. 56-69.

61. See Philippe Contamine, *War in the Middle Ages*, Michael Jones, trans., New York: Barnes and Noble Books, 1984, p. 77; Richard Preston, Alex Roland, and Sydney Wise, *Men in Arms: A History of Warfare and Its Interrelationships with Western Society*, 5th Ed., Ft. Worth, TX: Harcourt Brace Jovanovich, 1991, p. 59.

62. Felix Gilbert, "Machiavelli: The Renaissance of the Art of War," in Peter Paret, ed., *Makers of Modern Strategy from Machiavelli to the Nuclear Age*, Princeton, NJ: Princeton University Press, 1986, pp. 12-13. Preston, Roland, and Wise, pp. 69-71.

63. Gunther E. Rothenberg, "Maurice of Nassau, Gustavus Adolphus, Raimundo Montecuccoli, and the 'Military Revolution' of the Seventeenth Century," in Paret, ed., *Makers of Modern Strategy*, pp. 32-33, quoted material on p. 33.

64. Gilbert, pp. 21-22; Bernstein, "The Strategy of a Warrior-State," in Murray, Knox, and Bernstein, eds., p. 56; Heuser, pp. 84-85.

65. Gilbert, p. 24.

66. R. R. Palmer, "Frederick the Great, Guibert, Bulow: From Dynastic to National War," in Paret, ed., *Makers of Modern Strategy*, p. 91. See also Azar Gat, *The Origins of Military Thought: From the Enlightenment to Clausewitz*, Oxford, UK: Oxford University Press, 1989, pp. 1-9.

67. Rothenberg, pp. 34-36.

68. Gustavus Adolphus, King of Sweden and reforming general, ascended to power just a few years before the start of the destructive Thirty Years' War in Europe, 1618-48. Raimundo Montecuccoli, a field marshal of the Austrian Hapsburg army, was a noted reformer, administrator, and master of maneuver warfare. He fought in the latter stages of the Thirty Years' War.

69. Rothenberg p. 36. Scharnhorst considered Montecuccoli "an indispensible guide to the eternal nature of war." On Montecuccoli, see Gat, pp. 13-24.

70. Palmer, pp. 91-93; John A. Lynn, *Battle: A History of Combat and Culture*, Rev. Ed., Cambridge, MA: Westview, 2003, pp. 123-125.

71. Palmer, p. 91. For helpful general overviews, see Geoffrey Wawro, *Warfare and Society in Europe, 1792 to 1914*, London, UK: Routledge, 2000; David Kaiser, *Politics and War: European Conflict from Phillip II to Hitler*, Cambridge, MA: Harvard University Press, 1990.

72. Strachan, *The Direction of War*, p. 28.

73. Maizeroy quoted in *Ibid*. When the first two volumes of his *Cours de tactique, theoretique, practique et historique* (*Course in Tactical Theoretical, and Historical Practices*) appeared in 1766, Maizeroy was a lieutenant colonel in the French Army. His *Theorie de la guerre* (*Theory of War*) followed in 1777.

74. Palmer, pp. 113-119; Peter Paret, "Napoleon," in Paret, ed., *Makers of Modern Strategy*, pp. 123-142.

75. Wawro offers compelling insights into Napoleon and his era, see Wawro, *Warfare and Society in Europe, 1792-1914*, pp. 1-23.

76. Palmer, p. 117.

77. Strachan, *The Direction of War*, p. 29.

78. Brodie, pp. 1-2.

79. Thomas C. Schelling, *Arms and Influence*, New Haven, Yale University Press, 1966, pp. 1-34, especially p. 2.

80. Peter Paret, "Clausewitz," in Paret, ed., *Makers of Modern Strategy*, p. 187. Also, Strachan, *The Direction of War*, pp. 46-63.

81. On Jomini's influence, see Shy's masterful essay in Paret, ed., *Makers of Modern Strategy*, pp. 143-185. See also Strachan, who writes:

> His [Jomini's] ideas were plagiarised by military theorists across the continent, and they provided the axioms inculcated in the military academies which proliferated from the turn of the 18th and 19th centuries. His emphasis on planning, cartography and lines of communication meant that his definition of strategy became the *raison d'etre* and even justification of the general staffs which were similarly institutionalised during the course of the 19th century.

Strachan, "Strategy and Contingency," p. 29. Similarly, he argues, "These facets of Jomini's background conform with the self-image of the US armed forces, confident of their invincibility but also of the value of a rational and managerial approach to war." Strachan, "Strategy and Contingency," p. 1289. Also Gat, pp. 106-135.

82. Strachan, *The Direction of War*, pp. 31-33. On the rise of sea power and the influence of the *Pax Brittanica*, see Paul Kennedy, *The Rise and Fall of British Naval Mastery*, London, UK: Allen Lane, 1976; Geoffrey Till, *Modern Seapower: An Introduction*, London, UK: Brassey's, 1987; Geofrey Till, *Understanding Victory: Naval Operations from Trafalgar to the Falklands*, New York: Praeger, 2014; Preston, Roland, and Wise, pp. 104-156, 192-208.

83. For insights, see Tami Davis Biddle, *Rhetoric and Reality in Air Warfare: The Evolution of British and American Thinking about Strategic Bombing, 1914-1945*, Princeton, NJ: Princeton University Press, 2002, pp. 11-153; Richard Overy, *The Air War, 1939-1945*, Washington, DC: Potomac Books, 2005, Reprint Ed. See also the many excellent essays in Phillip Meilinger, ed., *The Paths of Heaven: The Evolution of Air Power Theory*, Maxwell Air Force Base, AL: Air University Press, 1997.

84. Howard, "Grand Strategy in the Twentieth Century," p. 3.

85. For an elaboration, see Preston, Roland, and Wise, pp. 212-216. Also Wawro. Enlightened essays on various aspects of this transformation can be found in Roger Chickering, Dennis Showalter, and Hans van de Ven, eds., *The Cambridge History of War*, Vol. IV, *War and the Modern World*, Cambridge, UK: Cambridge University Press, 2012.

86. The literature on World War I is immense. For a useful, perceptive, and brief summary, see Michael Howard, *The First World War*, New York: Oxford University Press, 2002. Other essential texts from recent years include Hew Strachan, *The First World War*, New York: Penguin, 2005; and Michael Neiberg, *Fighting the Great War*, Cambridge, MA: Harvard, 2009. See also David Reynolds, *The Long Shadow: The Legacies of the Great War in the Twentieth Century*, New York: Norton: 2014; and Heuser, pp. 179-183.

87. For perceptive insights, see Tooze.

88. See Max Hastings, *Finest Years: Churchill as Warlord, 1940-1945*, London, UK: Collins, 2010.

89. Maurice Matloff, "Allied Strategy in Europe, 1939-1945," and Clayton D. James, "American and Japanese Strategies in the Pacific War, in Paret, ed., *Makers of Modern Strategy*, pp. 677-732. For more insights on the Far Eastern campaigns, see Alessio Patalano, "Feigning Grand Strategy: Japan 1937-1945," and John T. Kuehn, "The War in the Pacific, 1941-1945," in John Ferris and Evan Mawdsley, *The Cambridge History of the Second World War*, Vol. I, June 2015, pp. 159-188, 420-454.

90. The argument is made in detail by this author in "Leveraging Strength: The Pillars of American Grand Strategy in World War II," *Orbis*, Winter 2011, pp. 4-29.

91. The phrase was first used by Churchill in his 1946 speech at Westminster College in Missouri.

92. Strachan has written, ". . . theories of deterrence were developed and employed . . . Deterrence itself then became the cornerstone of a new discipline, strategic studies, but strategic

studies were concerned not so much with what armies did in war as how nations used the threat of war in peace." *The Direction of War*, p. 36.

93. This was the central question of Samuel Huntington's classic 1957 work, *The Soldier and the State*.

94. For insight into Kennan's original conception of containment, see John Lewis Gaddis, *Strategies of Containment: A Critical Appraisal of Postwar American National Security Policy*, New York: Oxford University Press, 1982, pp. 25-54.

95. See Ernest May's introduction to National Security Council (NSC) 68 in *American Cold War Strategy: Interpreting NSC 68*, Boston, MA: Bedford Books, 1993, pp. 1-19.

96. Strachan, *The Direction of War*, p. 37. See also Tami Davis Biddle, "U.S. Strategic Forces and Doctrine Since 1945," in Andrew Bacevich, ed., *The Long War: A New History of US National Security Policy Since World War II*, New York: Columbia University Press, 2009.

97. See G. John Ikenberry, *After Victory* and *Liberal Leviathan*.

98. On the history of the Cold War, see John Lewis Gaddis, *The United States and the Origins of the Cold War*, Rev. Ed., New York: Columbia University Press, 2001; *Strategies of Containment*, Rev. Ed., New York: Oxford University Press, 2005; and *The Cold War: A New History*, New York: Penguin, 2006; Melvin Leffler, *A Preponderance of Power*, Stanford, CA: Stanford University Press, 1993; Melvin Leffler and Odd Arne Westad, eds., *The Cambridge History of the Cold War*, Cambridge, UK: Cambridge University Press, 2012.

99. The literature on Vietnam is vast, but notable volumes include: David Halberstam, *The Best and the Brightest*, New York: Random House, 1972; H. R. McMaster, *Dereliction of Duty*, New York: Harper Perennial, 1998; Frederick Logevall, *Choosing War*, Berkeley, CA: University of California Press, 2001; George Herring, *America's Longest War*, 5th Ed., New York, McGraw-Hill, 2013; and Lien-Hang T. Nguyen, *Hanoi's War*, Chapel Hill, NC: University of North Carolina Press, 2012.

100. Emphasizing civil-military relations, Strachan writes that:

> strategy was driven out by the wishful thinking of [the U.S. military's] political masters, convinced that the United States would be welcomed as liberators, and determined that war and peace were opposites, not a continuum. This cast of mind prevented consideration of the war's true costs or the implications of occupation, and the United States found itself without a forum in which the armed forces could either give voice to their view of the principles at stake or be heard if they did.

Strachan, *The Direction of War*, p. 45. For insights into the Iraq war, see, for instance, James Mann, *The Rise of the Vulcans: A History of Bush's War Cabinet*, New York: Penguin, 2004; Bob Woodward, *Plan of Attack*, New York: Simon and Schuster, 2004; Ron Suskind, *The One Percent Doctrine*, New York: Simon and Schuster, 2006; Michael Isikoff and David Corn, *Hubris: The Inside Story of Spin, Scandal, and the Selling of the Iraq War*, New York: Crown, 2006; Thomas Ricks, *Fiasco*, Reprint Ed., New York: Penguin, 2007; Emma Sky, *The Unraveling: High Hopes and Missed Opportunities in Iraq*, New York: Public Affairs, 2015. Also see Robert Jervis, "War, Intelligence, and Honesty: A Review Essay," *Political Science Quarterly*, Vol. 123, No. 4, Winter 2008-09, pp. 645-675; and Robinson *et al.*, especially pp. 24-29.

101. For official United States' statements on these threats, see *The National Security Strategy of the United States*, Washington, DC: The White House, 2015, available from *https://www.whitehouse.gov/sites/default/files/docs/2015_national_security_strategy.pdf*; and The Joint Chiefs of Staff, *The National Military Strategy of the United States*, Washington, DC: Department of Defense, 2015, available from *www.jcs.mil/Portals/36/Documents/Publications/2015_National_Military_Strategy.pdf*. For an insightful essay on the strategic complexities posed by the rise of China, see Adam P. Liff and G. John Ikenberry, "Racing Toward Tragedy?" *International Security*, Vol. 39, No. 2, Fall 2014, pp. 52-91.

102. Eliot Cohen, "Obama's COIN [Counterinsurgency] Toss," *The Washington Post*, December 6, 2009, p. 1.

103. Jervis adds, "As Henry Kissinger put it, "Historians rarely do justice to the psychological stress on a policymaker.... What no document can reveal is the accumulated impact of accident, intangibles, fears and hesitations." See Robert Jervis, "Serving or Self-Serving? A Review Essay of Robert Gates's Memoir," *Political Science Quarterly*, Vol. 129, No. 2, 2014, pp. 319-331, with quoted material on p. 331.

104. See Steven Metz, *Iraq and the Evolution of American Strategy*, Washington, DC: Potomac Books, 2008, p. xviii.

105. The large size of the present-day NSC may add to this challenge. Rather than functioning primarily as an organization overseeing and coordinating strategy, the NSC has become a major player in the interagency push and pull. See Robinson *et al.*, p. 45. For advice on possible reforms, see Dafna Rand *et al.*, *Enabling Decision: Shaping the National Security Council for the Next President*, Washington, DC: Center for a New American Security, June 2015.

106. See Paret and Howard, trans., *On War*, pp. 119-121. These pages are among the most insightful and enduring in Clausewitz's text.

107. For insights, see Jervis, "Serving or Self-Serving?" p. 323.

108. Betts, "Is Strategy an Illusion?" p. 7.

109. Robert Jervis, "Why Intelligence and Policymakers Clash," *Political Science Quarterly*, Vol. 125, No. 2, Summer 2010, p. 188.

110. For insights, see Betts, "Is Strategy an Illusion?"

111. Jervis, "Why Intelligence and Policymakers Clash," pp. 188, 190-195.

112. Matthew Moten, "A Broken Dialogue: Rumsfeld, Shinseki, and Civil-Military Tension" in Nielsen and Snider, eds., *American Civil-Military Relations: The Soldier and the State in a New Era*, pp. 42-71. Also Jervis, "Serving or Self-Serving?" p. 323; and Stanley McChrystal, *My Share of the Task*, New York: Penguin, 2013, pp. 316-361.

113. See Stephen Biddle, "Afghanistan's Legacy: Emerging Lessons of an Ongoing War," *The Washington Quarterly*, Vol. 37, No. 2, pp. 73-86, especially p. 82.

114. Betts, "Is Strategy an Illusion?" p. 7.

115. For an overview of this trajectory, see Rachel Maddow, *Drift: The Unmooring of American Military Power*, New York: Broadway Books, 2013.

116. Mark Bowden, "The Killing Machines," *The Atlantic*, September 2013, available from *www.theatlantic.com/magazine/archive/2013/09/the-killing-machines-how-to-think-about-drones/309434/*.

117. There is a large literature on this topic, but key recent texts include: Peter D. Feaver and Richard Kohn, *Soldiers and Civilians: The Civil-Military Gap and American National Security*, 2nd Ed., Cambridge, MA: MIT Press, 2001; Peter D. Feaver, *Armed Servants: Agency, Oversight, and Civil Military Relations*, Cambridge, UK: Harvard University Press, 2005; Eliot Cohen, *The Supreme Command*, New York: Anchor, 2003, reprint; Peter D. Feaver and Christopher Gelpi, *Choosing Your Battles: American Civil-Military Relations and the Use of Force*, Princeton, NJ: Princeton University Press, 2004; Marybeth P. Ulrich and Martin L. Cook, "US Civil-Military Relations since 9/11: Issues and Policy Development," *Journal of Military Ethics*, Vol. 5, No. 3, 2006; Thomas S. Szayna *et al.*, *The Civil-Military Gap in the United States*, MG-379-A, Santa Monica, CA: RAND, 2007; Nielsen and Snider, eds., *American Civil-Military Relations: The Soldier and the State in a New Era;* Sarah Sewell and John P. White, *Parameters of Partnership: US Civil-Military Relations in the 21st Century*, Cambridge, MA: Kennedy School of Government, Harvard University, 2009; Mackubin Thomas Owens, *US Civil-Military Relations after 9/11*, New York: Continuum, 2011; Betts, *American Force*, Chap. 9, "Civil-Military Relations: A Special Problem?" pp. 201-231.

118. Objective control in civil-military relations requires a delineation between the political and military realms, but this line can be blurred, intentionally or inadvertently, by civilian leaders or military leaders who either do not understand objective control or who may be caught in its very real challenges of implementation.

119. Betts explains that:

Both policymakers and soldiers have more than they can handle, working around the clock to deal with the demanding problems in their respective realms, with neither focusing intently on the linkage — the bridge between objectives and operations, the mechanism by which combat will achieve its objectives.

He warns that when the logic link is broken, strategy becomes "whatever slogans and unexamined assumptions" occur to them in the moments "left over from coping with their main preoccupations." Betts, "Is Strategy an Illusion?" p. 7.

120. Hew Strachan, "The Lost Meaning of Strategy," *Survival*, Vol. 7, No. 3, Autumn 2005, pp. 33-54.

121. Owens, "Strategy and the Strategic Way of Thinking," p. 115. He relates this to what Samuel Huntington termed "structural decisions," including organizational imperatives and proclivities.

122. There are many examples of the military feeling a need to justify a particular weapon; the history of the B-29 bomber, and its effect on the campaign in the Pacific in World War II, is one of many notable examples. For insights, see William W. Ralph, "Improvised Destruction: Arnold, LeMay, and the Firebombing of Japan," *War in History*, Vol. 13, No. 4, October 2006, pp. 495-522.

123. Robert Gates, *Duty: Memoirs of a Secretary of War*, New York: Knopf, 2014, p. 563.

124. Jervis, "Why Intelligence and Policymakers Clash," p. 195.

125. He wrote:

Like many soldiers of my generation, my ideal for how a military leader should advise and answer to a civilian, democratic authority had been drawn from Samuel Huntington's seminal treatise, *The Soldier and the State*. He argued a military commander should endeavor to operate as independently of political or even policy pressures as possible. And yet I found, as much as I wanted my role to be that described by Huntington, the demands of the job made this difficult.

See McChrystal, *My Share of the Task*, p. 351.

126. The details of the Truman-MacArthur crisis are explained well in Brodie, pp. 57-112.

127. See Williamson Murray, "Professionalism and Professional Military Education in the 21st Century," and Richard Kohn, "Building Trust: Civil Military Behaviors for Effective National Security," in Nielsen and Snider, eds., *American Civil Military Relations: The Soldier and the State in a New Era,* pp. 287-301.

128. Scott Sagan, "The Origins of the Pacific War," *Journal of Interdisciplinary History*, Vol. 18, No. 4, Spring 1988, p. 917.

129. For insights on how to maintain skills for post-conflict operations and stability operations within the military and how to organize them, see Richard Lacquement, "Professionalizing Stability Operations in the U.S. Armed Forces," J. Boone Bartholomees, ed., *U.S. Army War College Guide to Strategic Issues*, 5th Ed. Vol, II, Carlisle, PA: Strategic Studies Institute, U.S. Army War College, 2012, pp. 317-333. Also see Schadlow and Lacquement in Nielsen and Snider, eds., *American Civil-Military Relations: The Soldier and the State in a New Era*, pp. 112-132.

130. Steven Metz, "To Deter Adversaries, U.S. Military Must First Understand their Fears, *World Politics Review*, April 17, 2015.

131. Stephen Biddle, "Afghanistan's Legacy," p. 75. In a similar vein, H. R. McMaster, has written:

> If the indigenous government and its security forces act to exacerbate rather than ameliorate the causes of violence, the political strategy must address how best to demonstrate that an alternative approach is necessary to avert defeat and achieve an outcome consistent with the indigenous government's interests. If institutions or functions of the supported state are captured by malign or corrupt organizations that

pursue agendas inconsistent with the political strategy, it may become necessary to employ a range of cooperative, persuasive, and coercive means to change that behavior and restore a cooperative relationship.

H. R. McMaster, cited in Robinson *et al.*, p. 55.

132. Layton, "The Idea of Grand Strategy," pp. 56-61.

133. *Ibid.*, pp. 56-61.

134. Robinson *et al.*, outline seven imperatives for the improvement of strategic competence. See especially pp. 31-77, 93-109. See also David Barno, Nora Bensahel, Katherine Kidder, and Kelley Sayler, *Building Better Generals*, Washington, DC: Center for a New American Security, 2013.

135. Walter McDougall, "The Three Reasons We Teach History," *Footnotes* 5:1, Washington, DC: Foreign Policy Research Institute, February 1998, available from the Foreign Policy Research Institute website.

136. Biddle and Citino. See also Strachan, "The Lost Meaning of Strategy," p. 48.

137. Both the Smith Richardson Foundation and the Mellon Foundation have supported programs enabling this kind of very important educational interchange. Of particular note are the Smith Richardson-supported Summer Workshop on the Analysis of Military Operations and Strategy and the grants offered by the Mellon Foundation to support exchanges between civilian academies and institutions in the Professional Military Education system. In the spring of 2015, I was fortunate enough to co-teach a course, supported by a Mellon grant, that brought together 20 undergraduates from Dickinson College and 25 U.S. Army War College students. We used World War I as a lens for examining contemporary military, political, and social issues.

138. Jervis is critical of Gates for failing to fulfill this role as well as Jervis felt he might have done while Secretary of Defense, especially during the Obama administration. See Jervis, "Serving or Self-Serving?"

139. Michele A. Flournoy and Shawn W. Brimley, *Strategic Planning for National Security: a Project Solarium for the 21st Century*, The Princeton Project Papers, Washington, DC: Woodrow Wilson School of Public and International Affairs, 2006.

140. See Echevarria, *Reconsidering the American Way of War*, p. 47.

141. Betts, "Is Strategy an Illusion?" p. 6.

142. Walter McDougall, "Can the United States do Grand Strategy?" *The Telegram*, April 2010, available from *www.fpri.org/articles/2010/04/can-united-states-do-grand-strategy*.

143. No one has made this point more profoundly than Betts:

> Action is preferable to inaction only where policymakers think seriously beyond the objective and to the logic by which military means will take them there. Whatever the costs of refraining from war may be, they can seldom be greater than those from killing without strategy.

Betts, "Is Strategy an Illusion?" p. 48.

U.S. ARMY WAR COLLEGE

Major General William E. Rapp
Commandant

*****

STRATEGIC STUDIES INSTITUTE
and
U.S. ARMY WAR COLLEGE PRESS

Director
Professor Douglas C. Lovelace, Jr.

Director of Research
Dr. Steven K. Metz

Author
Dr. Tami Davis Biddle

Editor for Production
Dr. James G. Pierce

Publications Assistant
Ms. Rita A. Rummel

*****

Composition
Mrs. Jennifer E. Nevil

Printed in Great Britain
by Amazon

74284910R00057